Creative YOU TURN

9 STEPS
to Your New Creative
Life & Career

PAT PATTISON

BALBOA.PRESS
A DIVISION OF HAY HOUSE

Balboa Press books may be ordered through booksellers or by contacting:

Balboa Press
A Division of Hay House
1663 Liberty Drive
Bloomington, IN 47403
www.balboapress.com
844-682-1282

Because of the dynamic nature of the Internet, any web addresses or links contained in this book may have changed since publication and may no longer be valid. The views expressed in this work are solely those of the author and do not necessarily reflect the views of the publisher, and the publisher hereby disclaims any responsibility for them.

The author of this book does not dispense medical advice or prescribe the use of any technique as a form of treatment for physical, emotional, or medical problems without the advice of a physician, either directly or indirectly. The intent of the author is only to offer information of a general nature to help you in your quest for emotional and spiritual well-being. In the event you use any of the information in this book for yourself, which is your constitutional right, the author and the publisher assume no responsibility for your actions.

Any people depicted in stock imagery provided by Getty Images are models, and such images are being used for illustrative purposes only. Certain stock imagery © Getty Images.

Print information available on the last page.

ISBN: 978-1-9822-7031-5 (sc)
ISBN: 978-1-9822-7032-2 (e)

Balboa Press rev. date: 07/28/2021

CONTENTS

To Ruth, my life partner who inspired and encouraged me all the way, and who is an exemplary role model in her own career reinvention. I love you, sweetheart.

ACKNOWLEDGMENTS

THIS BOOK HAS A BEEN as much of a joy and a slog as my own Creative YOU Turn has been at times. As my creative career path changed and morphed along the way, so did this book. Both were "works in progress" and I kept learning and changing with them, which ultimately made for a better book.

At my side and giving me great support was my life partner Ruth Jacobson. She proofread, offered notes and helped hold the camera for my TV endeavors. My two daughters, Jessamyn and Liza, who share the creative gene, also chipped in with support as well as with technical and spiritual assistance. And my late wife, Jennifer Morris Pattison, was another compelling example of creative change and improvisation as she moved from being a Disney artist to being a garden designer in her second act.

Bob Dickman, my first coaching mentor, helped nudge me into the Hudson Coaching Community that solidified my "Creative YOU Turn" program into a life practice. Pamela McLean and her staff gave me the training necessary to help others in the specific way and methodology that is outlined in this book.

Others who lent a helping hand include my editor Michael Wolfe, my coaching workshop partner Jacqui Harper, Richard Eisenberg editor of "NextAvenue.org" and editor and TV producer Shirley Neal, who also helps with my TV shows. I'd like to give special thanks for the support and friendship of P.R. and branding mastermind Michael Levine, who helped keep me focused in the last mile.

I also want to acknowledge the example of my mother Lillian Pattison, who was discouraged from pursuing her art during an interview at a very young age with a very depressed Disney Studio bookkeeper. She was told to go to secretary's school instead, which she did, and yet she stayed CREATIVE her entire life. She always encouraged my siblings, Steve and Liz, and our own children to stay creative and work with our hands, and for that, I will always be grateful.

CHAPTER 1

Defining & Launching Your Creative Dream

"Every child is an artist. The problem is how to stay
an artist once we grow up." – Pablo Picasso

I'M RACING THROUGH L.A. TRAFFIC to get to the set of *Mystery ER*, a TV show that airs on the Discovery Channel. I've been called to play the role of a doctor, so on the passenger seat beside me sits a wardrobe bag with a lab coat and stethoscope. The casting director told me he really liked what I had done with the part in the audition and looked forward to working with me, and when I asked about the script, the producers had said not to worry, I would be improvising dialogue based on guidance from the director and the other actors in the scene. Sure, *piece of cake*.

There was only one concern crowding my mind as I weaved through Hollywood: I had been acting all of about three months. I had absolutely no idea what I was doing!

I had my acting "epiphany" playing Simon Cowell on stage in a skit at a trade convention. I knew I'd found something that gave me goosebumps. But what to do with it? Surely taking up acting at fifty-five wasn't practical. There are so many people doing it better, who have been at it longer and have all the time in the world to devote to it. To top things off, I lived in Los Angeles, the struggling actor capital

1

of the world. Where was my place and did I really have the energy for this? Did Hollywood really need another aspiring actor?

I threw caution to the wind, went to classes and learned how to submit myself for roles. At that point in my life, my overall goal had been a simple bucket list item of eventually getting to be on one national TV show with a line, or even to be an extra before I turned sixty.

Well, here I was, five years ahead of schedule with a substantial part on a cable TV show on a major network. I was scared to death. Like the dog that chases the car and finally catches it, I was asking, "How do I drive this thing!"

Fortunately, my friend Jenny is a TV actor and I was able to call her on my drive. "What do I do when I get to the set? What happens when my scene begins? What if I blow my lines? Should I tell them this is my first time?"

Jenny patiently guided me through the protocol of "action" and "cut", listening to the director only and NOT telling them, under any circumstances, that I was a TV virgin.

The set was huge and was the dedicated hospital set that the well-known TV show *House* was shot on. My scenes didn't come up for five hours after getting there, so I had nearly the entire day to worry about them. Finally, I was called to the set and was told what my scene was and who I would be working with. We shot scenes for about two hours and something kicked in that allowed me to relax and enjoy the process, be in the moment and improv with my fellow "veterans". If they only knew!

With this TV appearance, my career experiments had begun in full force and have continued ever since. I had taken specific steps to get to this pivotal moment of a Creative YOU Turn, and now I want to pass along those steps to you.

WHAT IS YOUR "CREATIVE YOU TURN" DREAM?

In his book, *Ignore Everybody: and 39 Other Keys to Creativity*, author Hugh MacLeod writes, "Everyone is given a box of crayons in kindergarten. Then, when you hit puberty, they take the crayons away and replace them with dry, uninspiring books on algebra, history, etc. Being suddenly hit years later with the 'creative bug' is just a wee voice telling you, 'I'd like my crayons back, please'."

Pablo Picasso is famous for his simplistic, almost child-like paintings, etchings, sculptures and ceramics. As an art major in college, I was blown away to see how he had nearly mastered traditional "realistic" painting and art by the time he was fourteen.

He was a highly trained prodigy. Once he'd mastered his craft, he spent the rest of his life simplifying his vision to be more and more simplistic, emotional and impactful. He succeeded better than anyone else in that particular genre and helped transform art in the twentieth century, and he did so in part by maintaining his vision of staying artistically creative like a child.

Perhaps you're thinking about retiring or switching careers, or you've lost a job and are trying to chart a new and more creative course. Maybe your children have gone off to college and you suddenly have more time on your hands. No matter what stage in life you're in, you might as well be doing something you're passionate about and really enjoy Whether it's a creative passion or simply being more creative in your existing career, this book will help you.

Being in Los Angeles, many of my career coaching clients are artists, animators, marketing executives, composers, film producers and novelists. They come to me with a need for remaking or refreshing their careers. In many ways they are at the same crossroads you may be at without even being in a creative career.

One client, whom I'll call Cathy, bought into the corporate dream. She faithfully toiled at her job, giving one hundred percent of her time and energy to the company, often at the expense of spending quality time with her family and friends. It was tough work, but she enjoyed it. After eight years, however, she lost her job. A victim of downsizing.

"What do I do now?" she pleaded during one of our coaching sessions.

"Tap into what you love most," I advised. "What is your creative passion? Acting? Painting? Music? Photography? Writing? Design? What is it that makes you want to get out of bed every day and do the work you're passionate about?"

She didn't have an immediate answer, but after carefully considering it she finally said, "I think I want to go back and do silk screening like when I was in college."

I could have responded with, "Are you out of your mind? You'll never succeed at that!" Instead, I said, "Cathy, that's a noble goal. Let's figure this out." I helped her put together a well-conceived plan of action that got her on the right path. Today, Cathy owns her own silk screen T-shirt business, and she couldn't be happier.

Cathy and I took the bold steps necessary to reinvent ourselves, and it paid off. We are not alone. A career study sponsored by AARP's *Life Reimagined* and *USA Today* found that half of those surveyed ages 45-59, would quit their current jobs tomorrow if they were in a financial position to do so. A third of the respondents anticipated making some kind of major career change in the future, and more than eighty percent of that group said the change would be driven by their desire to do something different, not by shifts in their particular industry or the economy in general.

If you've experienced a shift in your career, lifestyle, or an emotional crisis – job loss, retirement, divorce, death of a spouse, empty nest syndrome – I challenge you to tap into your creative career self and identify your dream. It can be freeing and rewarding. You owe it to yourself and to others who you might inspire with your gifts. You just never know how many people's lives you may touch.

Think about it – what if Martha Stewart had never made a Creative YOU Turn from stockbroker to Do-It-Yourself home guru; or Danny DeVito from hairdresser to actor/director? We would never have benefitted from their innate gifts. And they wouldn't be where they are today – not just successful, but happy! Instead of sticking with jobs that weren't fulfilling, they hit the refresh button. They challenged themselves to define their dreams, and then transitioned into careers that were more rewarding and that better suited their creativity.

My passion as a career coach and TV host is to help you use *your* gift to identify and attain *your* creative dreams. If your creative gift is buried, get ready to dig it up; if it's inactive, get ready to refresh it. I'll be guiding you towards making your own Creative YOU Turn, and I don't mean just fantasizing about a new creative life or career change.

A Creative YOU Turn is not an opportunistic diversion but rather a new mindset and lifestyle. For me, it's also been a spiritual journey of fulfillment. It's along the lines of Shakespeare's admonition: "To thine own self be true".

A Creative YOU Turn is available to anyone at any age. Being in the entertainment industry since I was twenty-three, I've had to reinvent myself a number of times. My most significant shift came in a very inconspicuous way when I was fifty-five.

One evening at a dinner, my friend Lisa asked if I could assist her friend who was looking for help with a skit for a trade conference.

"She could really use one more male performer," Lisa said, "if you're willing."

Really? Me? I thought. I was a Disney marketing executive, not an actor. My role had always been on the other side of the camera. For the most part, I was an "around the perimeter" guy.

"You'd be playing Simon Cowell in an *American Idol* spoof," Lisa explained.

Just as I was ready to say no, something inside me told me to consider taking contrary action. What the heck? I thought. What's the worst that could happen? At the very least, it was something silly that would get me out of the house. I said, "Sure. Why not?"

Lisa closed the deal before I could change my mind.

Leading up to the rehearsals, a day didn't go by that I didn't regret my decision. I was terrified. But as we went along, I surprisingly found my stride and started feeling fairly comfortable. On performance day, though, I was a wreck.

When it was time to deliver my lines in front of a real audience, my heart pounded. I clutched my index "cheat" cards that I planned to use only as a backup if I went blank during the sketch. I shook so much I could barely even read them. At one point, I completely forgot my surly Simon Cowell voice. "Gee, where did my fake British accent go?" I teased. And that got a big laugh. After a few more missteps and misreads, I got even more laughs.

I'm a hit! I thought. They're laughing.

The performance had become downright intoxicating. Turns out the audience liked us amateurs even more when we messed up. I experienced a huge sense of relief at that point and leaned into the joy of performing and being a part of a whole group instead of obsessing over myself as the center of attention.

When the skit ended, I walked off the stage to huge applause. It was an unplanned turning point that triggered a series of life-changing events. My Creative YOU Turn had officially begun.

That single experience eventually led me to the *Mystery ER* TV role I described earlier. Now, I've taken classes to become a professional actor and completed a prestigious program to become certified as a career transition coach, I've started my own coaching practice, hosted my own TV business talk show, appeared on numerous network news shows and even started my own TV travel series. I don't have a single regret about the decisions or sacrifices I've made that have helped to guide me along this journey, and you won't either!

UNCOVERING YOUR CREATIVE DREAM

As you embark on this journey and open yourself to the idea of a creative transformation, don't be surprised if you start to have new ideas come into your consciousness on a regular basis. In fact, you can come to expect it. Use this book as a workbook, but I'd write in pencil because things will definitely change! I find it's also a good idea to keep a notebook handy at all times throughout this process to capture your insights, or you can text them to yourself, because some of our best ideas come to us out of the blue. My other piece of advice is not to judge anything that comes into your head during this process. Just jot it all down. It doesn't mean you have to do it, but you don't want to risk the possibility of losing one of your best ideas because it was "stupid" or "too ambitious" or "never going to happen".

The process of self-reinvention is all about uncovering your creative dreams and taking action. It won't likely happen overnight, and it will only happen if you are true to yourself and that inner voice that you must coax out, but if you do a few simple things regularly, it will happen.

You're probably thinking to yourself, "That's great that it worked for you, Pat, but I'm totally overwhelmed and I don't think my life circumstances will allow me to just up and change everything. Where do I even begin?" That's exactly what this book is designed to do as a simple step-by-step plan. So let's get started with a simple, low-key exercise.

First, get as comfortable as possible, take a few deep breaths and then let yourself begin to daydream. Start by thinking about what your dream career or activity would be if you didn't need money to survive. What is the one creative thing that would make you want to get out of bed, day in, day out, to work on? Maybe you don't know what that dream job is yet, and that's perfectly fine at this stage, but I promise you'll have a clearer idea by the time you finish the exercises in this book. What's important now is that you start to plant the seeds for your Creative YOU Turn.

Let's begin:

If money weren't an option, I would _____.

I might also _____ or
_____.

And I've always wanted to explore (or learn more about) _____.

Now let's begin to define what's important to you and why. Your answers may change as we go along, but this is a good place to start and it will give you a reference point for many steps to come.

- What has kept you from starting this process before?
  _____

- What other obstacles are in the way of making this a top priority right now? (Money, children, health, etc.) _____

- What would help you physically to "make room" in your life?
  _____

- If you had to guess how long this might take, what is the outside time you will give for this to be in place? Be realistic. (Hint: it took me at least three years to get launched but I started having fun WAY before that time!) How much time per day or per week do you think you can devote to your YOU Turn plans?_____

- List any jobs similar to the career you seek that you have done in the past even if they were on a volunteer or pro bono basis. List any activity that has made you come alive in some fashion._____

- Who inspires you and is someone who "has what you want"? Mentor? Friend? Friend of a friend? Former colleague? Who has your dream life and vocation? If no one comes to mind who you know personally, someone you admire or have read about works just as well here.

_____

- Is there a group of people or someone you know who would help you on this quest? Church friends, school pals, co-workers, partner, creative mentor) If you can't think of anyone, imagine your ideal YOU Turn champion(s) and describe them.

_____

- List the skills and gifts you think you already possess that will help you to achieve this goal. (Writer, artist, highly organized, people person, etc.) Don't think too long and don't be falsely humble. This is your chance to shine!

_____

- How are you doing financially to support your new vision? How important is your current job to realizing your dream? Struggling currently? Be honest and keep the faith – we'll work more on this in Chapter 6!

_____

- List 1-3 steps you can take in the next week to further your plan and write down exactly when you'll do them and what your reward will be for accomplishing those tasks. (i.e. Go to a bookstore or library and find books on your vision, go shopping for a new Creative YOU Turn notebook, reach out to one of the Creative YOU Turn champions from your list to let them know that you're embarking on an exciting new journey and to ask them for their support going forward.)
  - _____
  - _____
  - _____

Congratulations! You're one step closer to defining and executing your creative dream. Now let's take that next important step towards your Creative YOU Turn and greater fulfillment and happiness.

CHAPTER 2

Creating Time & Space for Your Creative Dream

"Do What You Can, With What You Have,
Where You Are." – Theodore Roosevelt

HOW MUCH MONEY, SPACE AND time do you give your car? It's a non-optional necessity for many of us, and considering the finances alone, there's gas, insurance and maintenance, not to mention car payments and repairs. Spatially, I used to have a big garage and even an extra storage area where I kept car cleaning supplies, and that was just the space I devoted to my car.

Do you create space and time for the things that bring you joy? How about cooking or watching TV? Do you create space, time and budgets for these things? Is there a large pantry for your cooking materials and utensils or a TV room with sofa and chairs to sit back in and enjoy a game or a movie? How many streaming services do you subscribe to? These are both common activities that help us relax and enjoy life, and most of us don't think twice about the resources we put into doing either one of them.

Think about this: How much time and what kind of space can you create today to start enjoying the rest of your life in a creative and fulfilling way? As you re-center your life around your creative vision, pursuing your creative dream(s) should start to become as second nature as cooking and watching TV, and you will likely find that even creating a little bit of time and space will lead to more and more of both in a short period of time. In other words to paraphrase "build it and you WILL create!"

SPACE

My Disneyland buddy and concert tuba player, Stan Freese, is the ultimate expression of actually living within his art. He, along with our other former Disneyland colleague and artist friend Clare Graham, have created amazing examples of creative spaces that are worth making an extra side-trip for just to admire.

In Stan's case, he transformed his suburban home in Southern California into a mini-theme park of fun and musical creativity. Some people hang artwork to inspire themselves to stay in a creative mode. Stan and his wife Tera, however, LIVE in his musical inspiration.

It starts outside in his front yard with a California pepper tree filled with tubas and old Sousaphones. As you walk down the path to his front door, you encounter more sculptures and miniatures all with a musical theme. Once inside, you are surrounded by antique instruments, drums, banjos and more horns all tastefully hung on the walls or displayed about in various ways. It feels like you're in a very cool music school and you can't help but smile and want to pick up one of the instruments and start playing.

Now not everybody is as zany as Stan Freese or has a partner as cooperative as his wife Tera, but you get the idea. A little whimsy and good humor can do wonders to lighten the mood in a creative space, even if it's as simple as a silly figurine, a brightly colored accent or something on the wall that makes you laugh. In the beginning, I urge you to go nuts if you can. Create and live in a vision of all of the things you are learning in this book that help and inspire you. Just like when you were in school, this is your own private study area, but now it's all about creativity and fun.

Clare Graham has a famous space in L.A. called MorYork. It's a collection of hundreds and maybe thousands of Clare's found-object sculptures, assemblages and concept installations. MorYork is an impossible space to really get your head around and of course many years in the making. He uses it as a studio but also rents it out for special events.

Clare and Stan literally live inside of their creative visions. They are completely immersed, so that everywhere they turn they are inspired by or reminded of what they do. Again, not everyone has the ability to re-invent their entire space. We live with other people and have other facets of our lives that take up that space. My hunch, however, is that if you are new to a creative life, this is an area you might tend to neglect.

If you are a parent, how much space do your kids get? Are you constantly tripping over toys or moving old boxes of toys and clothes from one area of your home to another? Are they gone now? Are you still storing some of their things? When you look at space still being devoted to others it may be an indicator that prioritizing YOUR needs hasn't happened. Let's move YOU up the list now that the kids are gone.

When I looked around at the space in my home that wasn't being utilized, I realized that the only purpose my garage was serving was shelter for my car. I'm not a car nut by any means, and I'm fortunate to live in Southern California where the weather doesn't damage vehicles much at all if they're left outside overnight, so I ended up converting my garage into a small studio and office. It even has a small kitchenette so I can spend the night in my creative space when I want to. That one small sacrifice and change – parking outside – opened up an entirely new opportunity for me that has provided me with hundreds of hours of creative productivity and joy. I recognize that not everyone has a garage or can afford to convert one, but I'm almost certain everyone has an area to which they can dedicate their Creative YOU Turn project.

Most recently as I've launched a new TV show project I noticed a corner of my living room that I could convert into what is known as a "flash studio" in the TV world. This was a 6' x 6' area that I have screened off and have set up my recording equipment and "set" backgrounds to produce my TV project as needed. Because it is already set up I find I shoot my segments more often and in a more relaxed fashion.

Another friend of mine, Sandy, lives in a small one-bedroom apartment in the middle of Los Angeles, and when we started talking about his dream to get back to writing, he said he only had one table in his apartment where he had to do everything – work, eat, pay bills, etc. – so when it came time to be creative, it's the last place he wanted to be. When he took stock of the "negative" or underutilized spaces in his apartment, he considered emptying an entire closet before deciding instead to hang his bicycle by hooks from the ceiling to free up space for a standing bar and workstation on the wall he used to set his bike against. And it's right next to a window.

So, you can work within the space you have, but you have to get creative and you may need to compromise. To me, there is a direct correlation between your commitment to "claiming" your new creative life and how much physical space it takes up. Your creativity and the tools you use to create your dreams shouldn't be wedged into a corner, a dark closet or, still worse, stashed into a junk drawer like the old tired hobby that haunts you.

Remember, make it a place you long to be and where you can find your "zone". Are you a painter? Let your brushes out! A writer? Buy a new pen cup and fill it with some new pens. To help you declutter and make space, we'll take some time at the end of this chapter so you can "blow up" your current space and create a sacred new place for you to begin your Creative YOU Turn.

TIME

Now, what about time? This can be the REALLY hard part for many of my clients. After all, by definition, a "postponed" or "delayed" creative dream usually means, "I just never got around to it." It's like that great John Lennon quote, "Life is what happens while we're making other plans."

I started getting work marketing TV shows when I was twenty-three. I had my own department to run at The Walt Disney Studios, complete with an administrative assistant, by the time I was thirty. I was in hog heaven! I was making good money and I had a wife and young daughter to support. Because I was on the marketing side of things, I got to work with creatives in both the advertising industry as well as in the entertainment industry, so the job had many creative elements that more or less fulfilled me. I stayed on that track climbing the corporate ladder for a total of ten years. This is what's known as a "mink-lined rut", or getting too comfortable. There is absolutely nothing wrong with that and many people have the good fortune to stay in their positions until retirement. But, since you're reading this book, I'll assume you either want out of that rut or got thrown out of that rut.

Some years ago, I was at the Greek Theater in Los Angeles watching the great humorist Garrison Keillor perform his *Prairie Home Companion* show, and the famous actor Martin Sheen was one of his guests. Keillor asked him what he'd been up to, and Sheen said he was going to college for the first time (I believe he was sixty-six at the time). When Keillor exclaimed, "My God, you're going to be seventy when you graduate!" Sheen nonchalantly answered, "Well, I'm going to be seventy anyway."

When you think of finding and making the time to devote to your Creative YOU Turn, I want you to think about Martin Sheen. He had the perfect attitude… *If not now, when?* Just keep telling yourself "Well, I'm going to be XX anyway, why not have my creative dream too!

So, etch the idea deeply into your soul that you do have time. Take a deep breath, relax and move forward. As my beloved late wife Jennifer, a successful Disney artist, once wrote to me in a note: "You are not behind schedule – THIS is the new schedule."

To solidify the two ideas of creative space and time, complete this quick makeover worksheet:

SPACE:

- On a blank sheet of paper, using pencil, lightly draw an area in your house or garage that might become a dedicated space for your Creative YOU Turn. Locate it exactly as it is in relationship to your current existing floor plan. It can be a child's former room, space in the dining room or simply a card table set up in a corner of your apartment. Draw the furniture, bikes, desks or other items that may need to be moved around to create that dedicated space exactly as they are right now. Try to shoot for at least 6' x 6' worth of space, but for those of you living in smaller spaces, by all means do the best you can with what you have.
- Next, draw that same space but as you envision it once you're done with it. You might look at fun design and easy makeover ideas on websites like Pinterest to help inspire you to envision a truly special place.

TIME:

1. How much time can you commit to your makeover? Aim for three hours a week to start, which is thirty minutes a day, six days a week. But be realistic about your schedule – only you know what will work best. Tip: don't shoot for the moon on week one by saying you're going to devote eight hours a day to writing your new novel when you know you won't be able to commit to that.

    _____

2. When is your most productive time and how much time are you committing to your creative transformation each week?

    _____

3. What is the best reminder system you use to remind you take an action? (i.e. phone alarm, calendar, list, giant sticky notes, etc.)

    _____

4. What are the main obstacles that keeps you from doing good things for yourself? (i.e. kids, work, procrastination, etc.)

    _____

5. Who can you use as support to remind you to make this a priority? (i.e. creative mentor, friend, etc.)

    _____

6. Set your first creative date with yourself. When and where and what are you going to do? (i.e. I'm going to take myself to an art supply store on Sunday to shop for new markers, I'm going to check out a museum exhibit on Friday afternoon, I'm going to the bookstore on Tuesday after work to look for inspiring books in my new creative field, etc.)

7. I will start my Creative YOU Turn on (which day) _____ _____ at (what time) _____ by

(doing what) _____ for (how long) _____.

8. Write the following note to yourself and put it somewhere you'll see it:

    I COMMIT TO DEVOTING X HOURS THIS WEEK TO MY CREATIVE YOU TURN BY HAVING X (amount of time) SET ASIDE ON (at least three days) _____, _____ and _____.

    I WILL REMIND MYSELF AND MAKE SURE I DO THIS VIA _____.

    I WILL USE _____ AS A SUPPORT PERSON AND ALLOW THEM TO ASK ME IF I HAVE MADE MY COMMITMENT EVERY WEEK.

    I WILL NOT BE ASHAMED IF I COME UP SHORT, I CAN EASILY MAKE UP THE TIME ON ANOTHER DAY. THIS IS FUN, I'M ONLY GETTING STARTED!

CHAPTER 3

Rearranging Your Life Roles for New Creative Goals

"You can't connect the dots looking forward;
you can only connect them looking backwards.
So you have to trust that the dots will somehow
connect in your future. You have to trust in
something – your gut, destiny, life, karma, whatever.
This approach has never let me down, and it has
made all the difference in my life." — Steve Jobs

FOCUS & PRIORITIES

MY COACHING CLIENTS FACE TWO main obstacles when embarking on a Creative YOU Turn:

1. Being able to focus
2. Being able to prioritize time

Like New Year's resolutions, we all usually start off with great intentions to change what we do and how we do it, but life always seems to get in the way. Yet there are also plenty of people out there making a living creatively or living out their passions and dreams. What's their secret? Why does it seem to come so easily for everyone else?

Since I'm a child of the sixties and early seventies, rock 'n roll stars are a big part of my early hero worship. Growing up, it seemed like uncompromising artists such Bob Dylan, Joni Mitchell, Eric Clapton, John Lennon and Frank Zappa all had something in common. They appeared to have picked a role or a path when they were about seventeen or eighteen, followed that path with a dogged determination (mixed, of course, with incredible talent) and then: voila! They succeeded.

Well, guess what? That is exactly what happened! If you dig into biographies and interviews of this crowd, you'll find a few common traits they all shared: focus, prioritization of time, determination and a willingness to put their goals first. They all had a singleness of purpose to pursue their art and prioritized it. When a decision came up in their lives, their career, art and pursuit of success came first. And they never quit because they had a "Northern Star" to follow.

Bob Dylan and Joni Mitchell's histories in particular are prime examples of harnessing innate talent and then pursuing careers with such conviction and drive that their successes were nearly inevitable. Both of these artists were born and raised in desolate and isolated places (Dylan in Hibbing, Minnesota, and Mitchell in Saskatoon, Saskatchewan, Canada), where they toiled alone as outsiders and came up with personas that they willed into being. Dylan worshipped Woody Guthrie and Mitchell used a second-hand guitar with unique tuning to make herself a Canadian radio star by the time she was in her early twenties.

Both Dylan and Mitchell knew they had to leave their hometowns and head for New York or L.A. to make it big, and that their struggles and experiences along the way would simply make for more songwriting material. As far as I can tell, they were also both opportunists who would use people as needed and then move on in a guilt-free fashion. Sex, romance and occasional stealing of material weren't uncommon. I don't say this as judgement, just as an example of how they stayed focused on the "prize". They kept building their personae at all costs. They had created a story about themselves, and they prioritized the unfolding of that story in every aspect of their lives. In other words, life decisions were made to fulfill the story.

For many of us this "legendary story" just isn't our path and that's just fine. I will venture to guess though that if you think about it your life has a "theme" creatively. Mine was Disney, fine art, TV and Toys! What a stew to try and discern a calling from! Like you perhaps, my "dots" were a bit faint. Here's how we can try to bring them into focus.

WHAT'S YOUR STORY? INTERNAL & EXTERNAL.

I mentioned Dylan's and Mitchell's personas, and now I want you to think about your own. What's your story? Is it compelling enough to at least make YOU care? It seems simple on the face of it, but many of my coaching clients aren't so sure. They can see a successful path for others, but not for themselves.

Not everyone will be Eric Clapton or Joni Mitchell or Tiger Woods or the greatest genius in the field they aspire to excel in. We can, however, become better – and even the best – version of ourselves on our new chosen path.

We all have a story we tell others about our lives and careers. For the most part, it's easy to peg in terms of fairly universal milestones:

"I worked at this company for ten years."
"I got married at 22."
"I'm a mother with two children."
"I'm a lawyer/banker/real estate agent/salesperson/healthcare professional."

What's important to recognize here is that the story we *tell* is often different from the one we *hear* inside our heads. It may run in two directions. There is one that is proud of all of the achievements we've attained, like career, family, success, etc. And perhaps the one where we still yearn to do "something else" that's creative, purposeful, joyful, and mindful, such as: "I'm studying to be a yoga teacher." "My art just won and award." "I finished writing my first song!"

Then there's the story that pegs us as a certain "type" of person. The one that says, "I do this, but I don't do that."

"I'm not a musician; my brother is the musician in the family."
"I tried to paint or draw in high school and was pretty good, but I can't do that now."

Part of your makeover is to shed any negative or defeatist attitudes you have about yourself and your internal story. Regret and remorse are a complete waste of time. Sure, there are things you didn't do that you wish you had. There's no harm in looking back on your life. The trouble comes when you stare at it. Your inner story can affect who you can become, so be thoughtful and intentional about the stories you tell yourself about yourself.

FINDING YOUR LEAGUE

> "Harry doesn't mind if he can't make the scene.
> He has a daytime job, he's doing all right."
> — *Sultans of Swing*, Dire Straits

Some people get bogged down by comparing themselves to others who already seem to be enjoying the kinds of lives and careers they dream of having. Perhaps those seemingly successful people simply started earlier, or had other advantages that made it possible for them to do what they love for most of their lives.

To take an extreme example, there are a handful of fortunate individuals who get to play professional sports. There are physical limitations and all sorts of factors that go into whether somebody's good enough to go pro, but the percentage of actual major leaguers is minuscule compared to the overall population who want to play professionally. It's the same in every highly competitive profession.

For the rest of us, that leaves a much broader and too often overlooked category that I like to call the "Creative Minor Leagues". A tiny handful of people will achieve great fame and fortune in today's fine arts or design world, people like Jeff Koons, Frank Gehry or David Hockney to name a few. But there is absolutely nothing wrong with the minor leagues. A person who loves the game, whatever their game may be, can have a terrific time playing there.

Being a marketing and creative executive at Disney and elsewhere, I've worked with many visual artists in my professional life. I know many talented illustrators, designers, and photographers who have great jobs in the entertainment, theme park, toy, or other industries that need their skills. They simply do their fine art or passion projects on the side, staying very fulfilled while making a good living and providing for their families.

I'm not saying you should set your sights low and that you can't become a major league player in your new chosen field. But superstardom should not be the only thing you aim for, especially if you've decided to change direction mid-life. Otherwise, you're likely to miss out on the many wonderful, life-changing opportunities that can come to you if you are open to them.

That was the case with my unplanned acting career. I have not yet become the next George Clooney. The experience thus far, however, has been extremely rewarding in ways I never expected. And I know countless people in other fields who would say the same thing.

If we're lucky, one of the things we learn as we move forward in life is to appreciate what we have already accomplished while still pursuing the genuinely important things that we want to do next. As we set out to reinvent ourselves, we need to be flexible and attuned to what's realistic, logical, and doable.

In your journey to reinvent yourself, it makes sense that you might use your job, or loved ones, or current situation as a primary way of identifying yourself since they take up so much time. Plus, it's sometimes just an easier way for others to understand and categorize you when introducing yourself or getting to know someone. Interestingly, a British friend of mine shared with me that he can always identify Americans quickly because they tend to always start new conversations by asking somebody, "What do you do for a living?" In the U.K. and throughout Europe and other parts of the world, that's generally considered a breach of etiquette. "Americans seem to be more interested in what a person does than in who they actually are," he said. This fact may even pose a problem for you during a Creative YOU Turn process because others will want to quickly situate you in one professional or creative identity or another.

As our jobs and living situations change over time, our labels often morph from being the proudest of our lives to lifestyle labels like retiree, bicyclist or yoga addict. Consider the idea that if your identity is tied to your job, then perhaps it's tied to your ego as well.

Creative YOU Turn Transformation Story: From a Lawyer's Ego To an Adventure Traveler's Humility

I met Steve Kasher through a mutual friend. He is a great story on reinvention. When Steve attended cocktail parties, or even just talked to his in-laws, he used to love to tell people he was a lawyer, particularly if he was in a situation where he wanted to sound prestigious or puff up his ego... But that was before he lost interest in the law and had his Creative YOU Turn.

Originally from Omaha, Nebraska, Steve always had an entrepreneurial spirit. When he was just five years old, he'd take his lemonade-filled red wagon door-to-door instead of just selling it on the sidewalk in front of his house like most other kids. Once he saw how well that worked, he started selling old newspapers and magazines along with the lemonade. During his senior year in college, he wrote a book on how to get cheap airfares, and then sold them through college newspapers to earn extra money. Later, Steve went on to study law at UC Hastings in San Francisco.

Taking the typical route of what he thought success meant, he stacked up student loans, graduated, and worked as a litigator at a prestigious law firm for seven years. Then one day Steve had an epiphany: he hated his work. He didn't want to settle for a life he no longer wanted. Saddled with financial obligations that tied him to a paycheck, he didn't know what to do. So, he continued to work. Several months later, his wife, whose career was going very well, encouraged him to quit law and come up with a plan of action.

During this time, our country was experiencing a housing boom, so he decided to purchase real estate fixer-uppers and flip them for a profit. He loved calling his own shots and not being tied down to an eight-to-five job, but, unfortunately, due to his lack of experience as an investor, the venture never got properly off the ground and even lost money. For some people, "failures" are often the catalyst for a truer path and more successful or fulfilling calling.

It was at this point when Steve experienced one of the biggest stumbling blocks in a Creative YOU Turn, which is that he had to let go of his old self to make way for his potential self. This can be particularly difficult for those who have had careers in legal, medical, or other professional fields that required costly education or training.

With a failed real estate business, Steve put his ego aside and took time to reflect, and it was during that period of soul searching that he was able to let go of looking for a prestigious career and zeroed in on the one thing that he felt truly passionate about.

When I asked him what truly made his heart sing during one of our interviews sessions, he said, "I love traveling, and I really enjoy history and retelling historical stories. Stupid facts stick with me and I like sharing them with others."

Armed with that one realization, Steve chose to become a Tour Operator. To get his feet wet in the industry and learn the ropes, he started working at a travel agency. This commitment of time was very important in his process. Eventually, things really took off once he got a job as a guide for an adventure-tour company doing cross-country camping tours for post-college twenty-somethings from Europe.

"It was a blast, and it was that fun thing I had wanted to do," he said. "I felt like I had finally found something I was excited about and really enjoyed." Steve's little lemonade stand entrepreneurial spirit kicked into overdrive. "Then I realized there was a market for higher-end private tours, rather than most of the companies that fill people up in big vans and go off on on-site tours," he added. He started buying vans, and hiring tour guides and other staff to offer custom tours for families. It grew like wildfire from there. With someone taking over the day-to-day management, he was able to slide into a supervisory position. Steve's biggest challenge was creating enough business in the early days to make the tour company viable. Like with his other efforts, he struggled for a while. But he went into this one with his eyes wide open and more experience tucked under his belt, and it paid off.

Going from litigator to tour operator was a tough transition for Steve, but it was made easier once he disassembled his ego that had been connected to his old self and "pumped up the balloon" that was his new creative self. Since that time, Steve has sold his company and now does charity work in Africa.

FORGET THE PARACHUTE! WHAT COLOR IS YOUR BALLOON? AND HOW FULL IS IT?

Of all the exercises you will do in the book, this next one is my favorite and I think the most important. It has to do with the segments of life – how we spend our time and what we prioritize. It's also a very fun and visceral exercise. I encourage you to do it with somebody else if you can, and be sure to choose someone you trust and don't feel judged by. This is where you'll get to cut loose and take a long hard look at your aspirational self. This is about respecting your existing self, but allowing your new dreams a full room, literally, to sort themselves out.

THE LIFE FORWARD BALLOON EXERCISE

I can't take credit for creating this exercise, but I can enthusiastically recommend it. The Hudson Institute in Santa Barbara, California, where I was trained as a career coach, has an incredible program called Life Forward. It's an intensive few days that walk you through a series of exercises and workshops in large and small groups to get your life moving forward. In other words, it asks: where are you now and where do you want to be?

Part of the goal of this exercise is to address the whole person, not just the parts of the whole that we discussed earlier, such as: Mom, Lawyer, Marketing Expert, etc. For me, this exercise was the beginning of a journey that resulted in taking the incredible coach training at Hudson, which I can't recommend highly enough. Pam McLean, CEO and Co-Founder of Hudson Institute, has graciously allowed me to use the exercise here. It was by far one of the most effective life organizing exercises I've experienced.

Here's what you will need for the Life Forward exercise:

> 6 large latex balloons or blow up balls of any kind
> Black or colored Sharpie pens
> Balloon clips or tape
> 6 chairs or stands to move balloons around room

★ Or contact me at www.patpattison.net for a simple kit you can purchase.

OR

For the ultra-simple version, you can use:

6 chairs
Paper and markers to make life role signs
Tape for affixing signs to chairs

INSTRUCTIONS:

Preparation: Use markers to write the roles numbered below on balloons or sheets of paper, then attach to balloon stands or to chairs. These symbolize the various roles in your life. You will then begin placing these goals around you.

1. Personal
2. Work
3. Family
4. Couple / Partner
5. Friends
6. Community

The following is excerpted with permission from *LifeForward: Charting the Journey Ahead* by Pamela D. McLean and reprinted here to give you more information and ways to think about the various life roles.

As defined by the Hudson program, here are our primary roles along with the usual activities associated with them:

1. PERSONAL (SELF) ROLE

This is our core defining role and really is much more than a role. It is being connected to the core self that allows us to live a meaningful life. Activities associated with this role include:

• Intentional use of personal space areas at home and at work

- Care for the body and mind through good nutrition and exercise
- Continual cultivation if inner dialogue
- Personal time alone
- Personal self-care and nurturing
- Spirituality in whatever form you choose
- Reading and learning that supports personal growth
- Management of priorities
- Budget and money management
- Add others that are applicable to your life

2. COUPLE OR PARTNER ROLE

The care and feeding of your primary relationship. This, of course, is a very complicated up close and personal role with many challenges. Here are some of the activities associated with this role:

- Sign up for a class or two focused on developing your relationship skills
- Create regular times for talking through the tough stuff
- Talk and touch regularly
- Share roles, tasks, and fun
- Share projects and activities outside the home
- Engage in separate projects and activities outside the home
- Manage priorities
- Manage conflicts
- Create time for intimacy and sex
- Cultivate friendships with other couples
- Interface with each other's work commitments
- Manage shared health needs
- Budget and manage money jointly and regularly
- Develop recreation and leisure activities
- Engage in adventure, learning, and traveling together
- Add others that are applicable to your life

3. FAMILY ROLE

Your caring connections with children, parents, and extended family members. This is another role a part of you falls into (being a child or sibling) and a part of you chooses (parenting) for a lifetime. Parenting changes as children grow and often people find themselves also taking care of aging parents. People without children also have many shifts as parents, siblings, and extended families age and change. Some of the activities associated with this role are:

- New learning at every step of the way to support development of strong parenting skills
- Cooking and eating together
- Maintaining the home together
- Education of children
- Enjoying adventures and vacations
- Management of health needs
- Sports, activities, and hobbies
- Friendships with other families
- Spiritual development, ethics, and values
- Caring for parents
- Nurturing extended family
- At-home learning, lessons, and help

4. FRIENDS ROLE

Your caring connections with close friends and other acquaintances. Meaningful long-term relationships we freely choose in our lives require commitment, dependability, a listening ear, and an ability to engage and be present for another in good times and bad. Some of the activities with this role are:

- An evening outing, dinners, movies
- A long-distance telephone conversation
- Attending a sports event
- An annual golf, spa, or spiritual weekend

- A yoga class together
- A book group
- An adult education class
- Volunteer activities

5. WORK ROLE

Your job, career, or volunteer efforts to make a living and find meaning. Most adults spend more time in their work activity than any other role. In Western cultures, this role continues to erode our ability to adequately and fully engage in life. Work roles shift during our lives and many find themselves continuing to work longer to attain financial security and complete a final lap in their careers. Here are some activities associated with this role:

- Commuting or not commuting
- Completing work assignments effectively
- Career advancements and coaching
- Weekend assignments
- Work friends
- Leadership
- Business travel
- Management
- Supervising others
- Leading an organization
- Getting results
- Necessary career step
- Retirement planning

6. COMMUNITY

Your involvement in community organizations and activities. Our place in the broader society that has sustained sufficient order and meaning for our personal and family lives. At some point in our adult journey, most of us find some way to contribute something back to the world at large. Activities associated with this role include:

- Participation in community groups
- Membership in professional organizations
- Commitment to neighborhood
- Participation in social causes and political groups
- Volunteer activities in the community
- Participation on non-profit boards
- Awareness of the larger global community

Here's How to Use the Life Role model:

If you can, get a partner to help you with this exercise (if you can find a Creative YOU Turn partner who wants to do the same, even better!). Just be sure your partner is completely objective, non-judgmental, and doesn't impede you in your exercise. This way, you can stand in one place and have your partner "place" your roles where you tell them. You can place them yourself, but having someone else place them is preferable so you can focus more thoughtfully.

Step 1:

Gather the "roles" in whatever form you have chosen to use, then stand in a large open area (room or yard) and start the process of placing the roles where you feel they are in perspective to how you are living today. I find kitchens are a great place with not a lot of furniture and good flat tile floor to place the balloon stands on. Plus, it's a "homey" environment. You only need about a 6- x 10-foot area.

During this step, in addition to considering the actual time you spend in each role, it's also helpful to consider the amount of "head time" spent on that role. In other words, how "consumed" are you by this role?

Since I am assuming you want to change your current situation, it's important to look at what has you consumed and what you might like to change. For my clients, the most common one is either WORK or FAMILY at the expense of SELF or COUPLE. So, in this scenario, the WORK balloon would be very close to you and the SELF balloon might be far away. You get the idea.

Step 2:

Have someone take a picture of you and where your balloons or chairs are. If you are doing the exercise alone, just take a picture of your role placement. Capture this current scenario so you can compare it to the changes you want to make. If you can't take a picture, do a quick sketch of where these roles are.

Step 3:

This is where you *want* to go in your Creative YOU Turn life. Move the roles around. Experiment and play. Just like rearranging furniture, take time with each new configuration to see what feels right. Notice how one can crowd you and others need attention. Often this is a HUGE eye-opener for my clients and can even initiate tears.

Many clients wonder why certain roles feel immovable. Often work or family commitments. And why is PERSONAL so far away?

So, here's your chance. In a perfect Creative YOU Turn world, where would these roles go? Don't think about what others will say or how someone will or won't get by without ALL of your time. Just try to do the exercise without judgement and with your best life in mind.

Step 4:

Once you and your partner have placed the new life roles in place again, take another picture with or without you in it. I like the idea of a picture with you smiling amidst a representation of your new life roles configuration. You could even use it as a new screen saver on your computer or phone as a constant reminder. This new scenario is the key to having enough time, space, and focus to achieve your Creative YOU Turn life. Even if you don't use them as screen savers, keep your two life roles shots handy as you'll want to refer to them often as we progress.

CHAPTER 4

Test Flights: Creating Career Experiments

"You can't be that kid standing at the top
of the waterslide, overthinking it. You have
to go down the chute." - Tina Fey

AS A YOUNG GIRL, KATHRYN knew she wanted to be a psychiatric nurse. She even went so far as to write it in her diary when she was a teenager. "I'm not sure how I even knew back then what a psychiatric nurse did," she confessed. "I just knew I wanted to be one." That was around the same time she was cast in the lead role of her high school play.

Nearly four decades later, after a successful career in the medical field, then a failed marriage, Kathryn hit the REFRESH button on her life and career. Then, on September 18, 2005, she sat in a packed theatre in Hollywood, California, as she heard the words: "And the Emmy goes to... Kathryn Joosten for *Desperate Housewives!*"

Kathryn was elated! She had just won Outstanding Guest Actress in a Comedy Series – her first top honor for acting. She was sixty-six. The teenager who only dreamed of being a psychiatric nurse had arrived at the apex of her Creative YOU Turn.

"Some people in Hollywood think of me as a model for dramatic midlife transitions: suburban housewife to Emmy-winning actress. But

I never plotted a master plan for following my dreams" Joosten has said about her journey.

CREATING POSSIBLE SELVES

In her book *Working Identity*, Herminia Ibarra talks a lot about "possible selves" and the idea of experimenting with career options by actually doing them. She promotes the idea of setting up experiments to see if new creative career options work for you. Her "Test and Learn" model is exactly what I did for my Creative YOU Turn even though I was unaware of her model at the time.

She urges readers to craft experiments, which are essentially any actions that may unlock potential new paths or open up to other new experiences. By doing these experiments, you'll start to see your new "possible selves" emerge. She continues, "Once these possible selves begin to take form, we need to take more active steps to test the possibility more rigorously. Otherwise, we stay in the realm of daydreams." Last but not least, she urges readers to "change connections". As you design your experiments, you must reach out to a new network of people to help you facilitate your new career or creative endeavor.

In my own case, when I had my Creative YOU Turn at fifty-five, I designed and executed many career experiments before my passion of Career Coach and TV Host was fully realized and started taking shape.

One of the most telling experiences was testing my passion for acting. When I first got the acting bug and started taking some acting and commercial acting classes, it triggered "changed connections". I started meeting people who were more knowledgeable and better situated to help me explore my new career. Not only the teachers, but my fellow students, too.

I had it in the back of my mind that it would be very fun to end up being one of these "late bloomer" TV actors I always admired, just like Kathryn Joosten. People like Estelle Getty who played the cranky old Sicilian mom on *Golden Girls* got her first acting job at fifty-five and was cast on that hit show at sixty-two. After years as a graphic designer, the late Alan Rickman got his first film role at forty-two and went on to immortalize Snape in the *Harry Potter* series among delivering many other fine performances.

So there were reasons to believe that it was possible and that it wasn't too late for me. The first thing I did was enroll in acting classes for theater, film, TV, and commercials. I even took some Shakespearean acting classes. I LOVED Shakespeare, but I soon realized I wasn't exactly passionate about "telling a story" and didn't find myself dying to get to learn my lines or attend those classes. Not to say I won't want to do more classic acting later if the right opportunity comes up, but something else did emerge from these "learn by doing" experiments.

It turns out I photographed well on TV, and I enjoyed learning how to be on camera, something I never would have found out without the acting career experiments. With that information, I was able to focus on commercial acting and being an on-air TV host. Two to three years of more classes and progressively more rigorous experiments has brought me to a place where it is now my main area of supplemental income and fun.

Other experiments I used to get even more focused on my Creative YOU Turn were taking commercial jobs on spec for TV directors, doing extra work as a Cardinal on Ron Howard's *Angels and Demons*, taking the part of a priest in a low budget independent film, being the "bare chest" on an operating table in a political ad, doing print modeling work for a clothing company, being a testimonial for mattresses on an infomercial, being on a rock star's reality show, and more. All of this combined led to two pivotal projects: A national pharmaceutical commercial that made me eligible to join the actor's union and the opportunity to host a local cable show where I conduct interviews with people re-inventing themselves.

I get booked occasionally for national TV ads, which is a great income stream, and my TV hosting experience has led to various other TV projects, not to mention this book. And another side opportunity emerged when my on-air work eventually got me some print modeling work which has become yet another fun opportunity and source of income.

All of this activity came about because I was willing to explore a "possible self" of being an actor and taking the steps to try it on for size. I stopped saying "no" and started saying "yes".

CAREER-ADJACENT EXPERIMENTS IN YOUR OWN BACKYARD

I'm going to use two examples of people who've had great success in their careers and have had an incredible amount of fun doing it. One person was forced to experiment with new roles in their existing field; the other person was able to invent a whole new job category for himself. Both cases show how your Creative YOU Turn may be closer than you think.

The Tuba Czar

Remember Stan Freese, my Disney buddy from Chapter Two? The one with the tubas hanging in a pepper tree in front of his house? He's a perfect example of career experiments and staying open to where they can lead.

Stan likes to say, "Life's too long not to have fun!" And his career is a testament to that very profound statement. Stan's forty-two-year stint with Disney began as the leader of the band that marches down Main Street at Walt Disney World. Then he got transferred to Disneyland in Anaheim where he did that job on and off for a number of years. He eventually became the Talent Booking Director for all the musical talent that plays in the Park before just recently retiring.

Stan got to where he is today with a great deal of talent and an amazing ability to grab hidden opportunities when he saw them. There's no roadmap on how to do that, or a way to study that in school, but he would tell you he did it by *always saying yes*.

His exemplary career began as a high school music teacher in Minneapolis, Minnesota. He's been on *Hee Haw*, has toured the world with Philharmonic orchestras, and has been showcased on numerous rock and contemporary music albums. So, throughout the years, Stan collected one of the most robust contact lists of anybody in the entertainment industry.

But life could have taken a completely different direction when he almost turned down an invitation to play in Russia (which eventually ended up getting him a gig playing tuba for President Nixon at The

White House). The State Department *strongly* requested that he show up, and ever since then he's always said yes to every opportunity that has come his way. His story landed on the front page of the *New York Times*, and it was that article that ultimately launched his Disney career.

As you go through this process, think about what exists in your own backyard that can lead you to opportunities and experiments. You may be in the banking industry, a stay at home mom, in the real estate industry or in manufacturing. Maybe it's volunteer work in your community, or a job at your church or your kids' schools. There are many opportunities within reach that can help you get closer to your goal. Like Stan, if you say "yes" to these nearby opportunities, you'll be much closer to achieving your goal. There's no reason to wait to start saying yes.

The Viral YouTube Video Prankster

Another great example of "career experiments" that evolved into a full-time passion is actor Greg Benson's journey.

Greg grew up in Texas and eventually moved to Los Angeles to become an actor. He did one of the riskiest things a budding actor could do: he flipped the switch and quit his job as a waiter to devote his efforts full-time to acting, and he's had great success doing industrial films and national commercials ever since.

One of his passions was doing sketch comedy videos (the type you'd watch on *Saturday Night Live*). Because it was always something he had wanted to do, he funded and produced them himself while doing other work, and then posted them on various social media networks at the time such as MySpace and YouTube. When the budding platform YouTube put one of his prank videos on its front page, it was all Greg needed to launch his new venture. Now, his "Mediocre Films" YouTube channel has over one million subscribers and some of his prank videos have received over twelve million views!

I use Greg as an example because he created his job rather than choosing an existing one. Thanks to the digital age, there are many kinds of careers available today that previously didn't exist or no one had thought to do. The world is literally your oyster, and your creativity and imagination is the pearl inside!

YOUR PATH ONLY NEEDS TO MAKE SENSE TO YOU!

These two highly talented, creative individuals ended up with jobs that suit their personalities and lifestyles to a T. So what can you learn from their experiences?

Both men made very practical decisions while devoting themselves wholeheartedly to what they wanted to do. In Stan's case, he lived and breathed his job while raising two sons. Greg partnered with his wife to turn a hobby into a career, and YouTube just happened to be new at the time and eager for material like his. He was at the right place at the right time, and he took a leap of faith. Both Stan and Greg were able to expand their creative passions while pretty much staying within their existing careers, so their experiments were a bit less risky and had a built-in safety net since they weren't leaving their day jobs.

Are these unique people in unique situations? Maybe, maybe not. But one thing is evident: they never wavered from what they wanted to do. They asked for what they wanted and pushed their own creative agendas to achieve it.

Because they believed in themselves and were willing to take risks (of course, using some very sound judgment while laying the groundwork for their future), they've lived lives full of purpose, passion, creativity, and great joy. I'd say that's not bad at all.

TAKING ACTION

"Identities change in practice as we start doing new things (*crafting experiments*), interacting with different people (*shifting connections*), and reinterpreting our life stories through the lens of the emerging possibilities (*making sense*)." — Herminia Ibarra, *Working Identity*

The best way to get a career experiment off the ground is to simply get started. Go online and search for various companies you'd like to work for (whether it's a Hollywood studio like Disney, a creative or artistic endeavor, an online retail business, a restaurant, etc.), and look at their job openings.

As you read through the descriptions, think about what it would be like to be a consultant for those jobs. This worked very effectively for me. During those times when I went from being a corporate employee to being self-employed, the transition from one to the other usually came via consulting.

If you're a budding Web designer, photographer, sculptor, painter or writer (or whatever your aspiration is), you can get a firm idea of the qualifications you'd need and then design your consultancy firm to get your foot in the door.

All businesses and jobs I've been involved in became one opportunity leading to another because of the training I gained from each position (though some of the basics can be learned in school). And the thread connecting all of them proves you can establish your own niche.

Case in point: my experience in the entertainment industry. I first started in local TV (KTTV-Los Angeles) as an ad director, which meant my job was to write headlines and copy for *TV Guide*. I'd also write voiceover copy for the person announcing the next program while credits rolled at the end of a TV show. I had no idea this kind of job and promotional world in the television industry existed. But had I given it some thought, just like motion pictures are advertised with posters, commercials, and tie-ins such as McDonald's Happy Meals, I would have realized television shows got the same treatment. It is an area of entertainment marketing that's since grown more sophisticated with technological advancements.

This experience segued into getting more local TV jobs and then a job at The Disney Studios as a VP, and finally at Disneyland where I learned how toys and merchandise were designed not only for the theme park, but for all the entertainment tie-ins and promotions.

From there, I owned my own business for ten years creating merchandise for various entertainment entities, one of which was a hugely successful program for the Chiat\Day advertising agency to develop car antenna balls for the Jack in the Box fast food chain. Then, I took a position with Applause Toys, where I became involved in licensing for fast food happy meals. I worked with movie studios on merchandise tie-ins such as *Star Wars* and *Lord of the Rings*, and I gained another expertise I hadn't known about before. After the licensing stint, I created my second business, Incentive Plus Network, where we did contests and merchandising programs for TV shows like *America Idol*, *The Voice*, and even the Super Bowl! As you can see, one stepping stone led to another, skipping me across the big river of my constantly evolving career.

CREATING "LOOKS-LIKE" EXPERIMENTS-YOUR PROTOTYPE

In toy manufacturing and marketing, we created "looks like" samples, which were essentially items very close to what we wanted to create or, in the case of advertising, templates that were similar to where we were headed on a particular promotion. We custom created non-working prototypes or rough layouts that had the look and feel of an item we were contemplating making.

All of this effort was a way to explore the viability of something prior to investing the time, resources, and cost of actually making something final, and it's a huge tool for you to add to your Creative YOU Turn arsenal. Since many of us are taking this step a bit later in life, it may not make sense to go back to school, train, and try to get a job only to find out that once we are in the exciting new role we can't stand it!

The first priority is to try and do experiments in the exact creative endeavor or job you want to end up in. Barring that, you can create "looks-like" experiments that come as close as possible. In other words, getting the freelance writing job for your local newspaper's website might be a stretch while you polish the creative writing skills you haven't used since college, but what about the newsletter at your place of worship, a community theater you frequent, or your favorite charity? It might be paid or pro bono, but either way you get a "free" chance to see if you want to pursue this new venture.

A favorite acting teacher of mine taught me every audition I go on is a free acting lesson. It can be the same with your "test flights". Don't worry so much about success or fail, it's about learning and experiencing. You get a chance to experience what is ACTUALLY involved in the path you're considering and not just the fantasy or speculation. It will save you an incredible amount of time in the long run, so take it seriously, but, by all means, have fun!

CAREER EXPERIMENTS WORKSHEET

1. **Jobs I want to experiment in** (in descending order of interest) (i.e. TV writer, journalist, marketing, technical writer, etc.):

    _____

2. **Companies or organizations I want to experiment in** (i.e. Disney, Habitat for Humanity, SpaceX, neighborhood yoga studio, etc.):

    _____

3. **New connections** (People who can help me get my experiments started or know people who can help):

    _____

4. **Actions I can take to learn more about these careers and/or companies** (i.e. take a class, call a friend, enroll in a workshop, etc.):

    _____

5. **"Looks-like" experiments I can explore immediately** (i.e. photographer or writer for church newsletter, marketing for a grandchild's school, online blogger for a non-profit, etc.):

    _____

6. **Experiments I can pursue long-term** (e.g. Part-time volunteer, shadowing someone on a job, part-time assistant for a job I want):

    _____

7. **What will I do today to get my creative career experiments started?** Later this week? This month?

    _____

CHAPTER 5

Welcome Home: Finding Your Creative Tribe

"Everyone is born creative; everyone is given a
box of crayons in kindergarten. Then when you
hit puberty they take the crayons away and replace
them with dry, uninspiring books on algebra,
history, etc. Being suddenly hit years later with the
'creative bug' is just a wee voice telling you, 'I'd
like my crayons back, please'." — Hugh MacLeod,
Ignore Everybody: and 39 Other Keys to Creativity

ONE OF THE HARDEST PARTS of a Creative YOU Turn is following through and maintaining your enthusiasm for the challenging road ahead. This can be particularly true if you are making an about-face and starting from scratch in a completely new field or business category. Where is your support? How do you avoid being discouraged or bumped off track? Who can you trust to give you some objective input?

When I got the acting bug at the age of fifty-five, I was afraid to take classes because I'd never really been a great student. School just didn't come naturally for me – I tended to get bored quickly and lacked good organizational skills. I managed to get decent grades, but it was a grueling enough process that I eventually dropped out of college. Luckily, I landed a job in TV marketing and advertising that led to my great career at Disney and entertainment marketing, so not having a degree worked out for me, but school-type settings still intimidated me.

I knew that I had a short attention span and learned best by doing, so I realized that jumping into an acting class where we immediately started performing would be perfect for me. There wasn't a lot of lecturing or homework other than learning lines. But when I was thrown in front of a camera to see if I could do a "bite and smile" (biting into a candy bar and smiling into the camera authentically and effectively), I became very self-conscious, nervous, and stiff.

Realizing the class was full of people who had varying degrees of comfort, expertise, and experience with acting allowed me to accept that I was new and didn't need to know what I was doing, which was a wonderfully liberating experience. Part of it may have been my age, because I didn't care if I looked like an idiot, and I had no expectations other than pure enjoyment. So it's helpful to remember that the adventure you're about to embark on might simply be for sheer pleasure; it's a bonus if it can earn you a living.

PERMISSION TO BE A NOVICE & OVERCOMING PUBLIC HUMILIATION

Finding good acting classes and supportive teachers allowed me to navigate the rough patch of being a "novice". Being a beginner can be very hard for people at any age, but exploring something later in life can offer up its own set of difficulties especially in terms of flexibility and teachability.

It was hard for me to find an acting teacher I was comfortable with. I went through a couple of classes that had self-described "tough" teachers who were going to show us how hard the acting world was and toughen us up with cold intimidation and not a lot of compliments. We were scolded for our appearance, our posture, being late, and so on. It reminded me of gym class in high school and I didn't like it. It may be just what a new twenty-something actor needs, but it really discouraged me.

Eventually, I found two older veteran teachers who were perfect for me for different reasons. Deborah Strang at A Noise Within, a classical and Shakespeare theatre based in Pasadena, Caliornia, was very welcoming and struck just the right balance of being supportive, fun, and serious. Mark Teschner was an Emmy award-winning casting director for *General Hospital*, and although he had a gruff, no-nonsense exterior, he made audition scenes fun and knew how to show us the essence of the emotion and action we were after as actors. He talked straight and didn't humiliate us, and those were key attributes for me as an adult student of acting.

My first class with Deborah is worth recounting because it introduced me to the concept and practice of letting go of any pretense in acting. Before you can get into her class, you have to take a Reading Shakespeare class which is designed to familiarize students with the Bard's language and Elizabethan England. So I started the Acting Shakespeare class with twenty other people, many of whom had been doing this a long time, and a few older, "second-act" people like me. I was very nervous, but Deborah put us at ease by leading us in some body exercises on the big wooden stage.

I should mention here that I am prone to allergies, and the first class took place in the spring. The pollen had me in sneezing fits. One of the allergy treatments I use is a Neti pot, which is a holistic remedy from India that affords a way of irrigating the sinuses with a diluted saline solution to help keep sneezing to a minimum. It works great, but occasionally some of the liquid stays trapped inside your sinuses and only comes our when your head is tilted at a certain angle.

So there I am starting my first Shakespeare class excited and nervous. As we start our body exercises, Deborah directs us to bend over from the waist and let our heads hang down toward the floor, then slowly come up with our eyes closed and swing our upper torsos around. No problem, I got this, I thought. Except I had used the Neti pot earlier that day and as I brought my head up – *whoosh* – out came a nose blast of salt water all over the stage floor! So much for having any pride and decorum! I cleaned it up and moved on with the class.

Too much information!? I'm hoping it makes anything you experience look like small potatoes. After the nasal escapade, I was able to pretty much let anything happen and not be too embarrassed from that point on. In the end, it was the best thing that could have happened to me!

I'm not saying you have to have this type of episode in your early "Creative YOU Turn", but for me, this type of "ego-release" was a good one and served me well. It allowed me to admit where I was in the process and to get in the habit of seeking help and support along the way. In doing so, I learned how not to take myself so seriously as well, which is something I constantly remind myself and my clients: don't forget to have fun!

Another great way I found to make the journey fun was improv! I found that after many classes and auditions it was still hard for me to cut loose and be free. My actress daughter has always taken improv classes and even taught it, but it always seemed WAY too scary for this novice.

Once again it just took the right teacher with a gentle and encouraging touch for me to jump in. Paul Hungerford at Keep it Real acting nudged me along with his zany and yet also serious style and program. His ability to create a safe space for what is a very intimidating experience was magical.

To be honest I thought I'd be a natural at improv since I'm told I have a quick wit and humorous mind. One-liners come fast and furious to me as well as smart-aleck zingers. To my surprise that didn't help a bit. It turns out that improv is all about being present and listening. Paul taught us techniques of active listening and going with the flow which proved invaluable in my acting and particularly auditioning.

No matter what your "Creative YOU Turn" is you might consider some form of improv class to achieve that same sense of openness to reacting, listening and "the now" that Paul helped me achieve.

AVOID TOXIC PEOPLE & TURN TOWARDS THE LOVE

How often have you heard: "Why would you do that?" "You don't strike me as *that* type of person." "Isn't it a bit late to get started doing that?" "How will it pay?" Or something similar? Make a mental note of who has said these types of things to you in the past and, when it comes to your Creative YOU Turn, avoid discussing it with them at all costs. The worst offenders might even be some of your own family members.

Friends and family like to pigeonhole us. They put us into a certain category and keep us there. This isn't always true, but, in my own case, I simply found there were two types of people I could talk to about my new career dreams:

> Type 1. People who made me feel better when we were through talking

> Type 2. People who made me feel worse and created doubt about my plans

Pretty simple categories, right? Now, I'm not saying we want smoke blown in our face about the reality of what we are up against, but I am suggesting that you need to be discerning about who you talk to. Stick with people who "get it" and support your plan or have done it themselves. That usually means like-minded people or ones who might already be doing what you want to do. This is your TRIBE.

If you are so positioned, I strongly recommend investing your time and resources in some kind of mentoring or coaching for your journey. In some cases, you may even be able to find this type of situation for free, say, for instance, you connect with a local writing group or photography club. We'll get into "magic people" in a later chapter, but in the meantime, ask yourself: what person or group of people immediately comes to mind who are supportive of you?

Make a date to meet with them on a regular basis. I have multiple support communities. My coaching school, Hudson Institute, has great resources for graduates that keep us connected and up to date on the latest trends in the coaching field. They also host webinars, and I have regular lunches with other graduates in the L.A. area. Aside from my Hudson Institute community, I'm a part of a small art salon that meets every other month to discuss and review creative projects we are working on. I also have a spiritual community I'm a part of, which is a support group I meet with around two to three times a week. In fact, I have so many support groups and mentors, it's a wonder I have time to write, coach or work on my TV projects!

I couldn't do it without them though. I grew up with a lot of emotional support about creative things, but it stopped there. What I needed were people who could help me design and execute a plan to make a living with my art, which is a whole different level of expertise. You, too can access these opportunities in your life. There are individuals and groups out there just waiting and eager to embrace you.

VIRTUAL SUPPORT IS GREAT, TOO!

I got my feet wet in the digital space about ten years ago when I started using Constant Contact for my TV Marketing business. I would send out newsletters and updates and I could track what was of interest, who opened them, what subject lines worked, and all sorts of other magical data. For someone raised in mass media and TV, the feel of this one-on-one interactivity was intoxicating. I was hooked. Within two years, I had a database of over eight thousand TV industry people I communicated with regularly. One of the huge benefits of this is that these people know who I am because of my online visibility and interaction with them via email, so then when I showed up at trade conferences, they'd see the guy who'd been sending them a newsletter every month and say hi. And it still happens to this day.

Is this a support community? You bet! And you can build your own in a similar fashion. When I started my Business of Art class, a student asked if we could start a Facebook page for the class so we could talk to each other and post assignments, photos, art we'd completed, etc. It made my life a lot easier as a teacher. Then, when I expanded my class to my coaching practice, I opened that Facebook page up to include anyone who was looking to be "remade" creatively. It soon had over seven hundred likes and has become a thriving community that I can regularly engage with, as a teacher, a coach, and as a fellow businessman and artist. It's been a huge asset in my arsenal. Social media groups are a quick and cost-effective way to find people to interact with you in your new creative endeavors.

One of my latest TV projects, "The Best of California with Pat Pattison" series, was even launched on Facebook. It allowed me a low barrier of entry to explore a new concept that had grown out of a friend's "Best of Los Angeles Award" platform. So, as I hosted video segments for the "Best of L.A.", I also produced my own segments for "The Best of California". It's been my most exciting project to date and has evolved into a national TV show. It's been a blast, allowing me to travel as well as indulge my passion for history. I've already covered everything from a transgender auto CEO scam in the 70's to the mating habits of the elephant seals in San Simeon near Hearst Castle!

I also love LinkedIn as a tool for business. Of course, it's ideal if you're looking to get a job, but you can also use it as a way to have quick conversations and get immediate feedback. I have found partners for some of my TV projects and even gotten one of my agents via LinkedIn's business service. One of the great benefits is you can search categories of like-minded people. For me, that's usually casting directors, TV agents, and other coaches, producers, actors or models. Recently, I've been curious about volunteering to coach in senior living residences and have turned up many people in that industry. It's an easy and quick way to connect with people and proves the Internet is truly a place to "net" work.

Instagram, Pinterest and Mectup.org are other great ways to go for creatives. ZOOM during the pandemic is another example of tech coming to the rescue and then turning into an essential tool. Regular audio-only phone calls just don't cut it for me after a year of ZOOM calls. And I'm sure by the time this book goes to print, five new services will have been launched and on their way to being the next big thing. Even though it can be intimidating, I encourage you to remain open to all of this new technology and view it as you would any other creative tool. How can each new technology or website best work for YOU?

The main idea here is to simply get started with a community you can embrace and that will embrace and support you in your new creative life. Let's list how you can get that going:

1. List three supportive people within your close friends or family you feel safe with:

   _____

2. List toxic people you should avoid talking about your Creative YOU Turn with at all costs. (These can be well-meaning friends, but you should just not go to them with this part of your life. I call that going to the same well expecting different water. Just don't do it.)

   _____

3. List a class, support group, 12-step group, church, temple or any other kind of group you can safely go to with your "plans and dreams":

   _____

4. List two or three people you may not be too close to but always make you feel better about your aspirations (losing weight, work, family issues). This could include a counselor, teacher, coach, priest or anyone you can talk to.

   _____

5. What social media or digital tools can you use now or get trained to use for your Creative YOU Turn?

   _____

6. Now, list five things you can do this month to start utilizing your support network (in-person meetings, phone calls, simple networking, internet community research, ZOOM, etc.) All of it will add up to keep you inspired and on track!

   _____

CHAPTER 6

Finance Your Dream & Build a Montage Career

"What we really want to do is what we are really meant to do. When we do what we are meant to do, money comes to us, doors open for us, we feel useful, and the work we do feels like play to us." — Julia Cameron

I WISH I COULD SAY mine was a well-oiled plan that I had executed flawlessly. The truth is it all came about by luck, necessity, and some tough financial times. I was the head of licensing for the Applause Toy Company and had just wrapped up the licensing for a line of *Lord of the Rings* and *Star Wars: Episode 1* toys we had planned to launch at the beginning of the new millennium.

It was 1999, the era when Yahoo bought Broadcast.com for $5.9 billion, Mattel bought The Learning Company for $3.5 million and sold it a year later for $27.3 million, and the Pets.com puppet took the internet by storm. One day, some whip-smart, stock market-savvy, tech-types came to Applause to present to our senior management team and show us how we could start selling all of our products on this new internet thing and easily get the company valued at over a billion dollars in no time. We simply had to make an IPO and didn't even have to be profitable. To say it was a roller coaster is an understatement. Applause bet the farm on many new ideas but was unable to maintain

49

itself. Ultimately, it had to be liquidated to its former owner Bob Solomon, who tragically committed suicide three years after he bought the company back.

I was caught in the crosshairs of the whole thing and out of this morass I found myself at a fork in the road. The ever-volatile Solomon had fired me at the New York Toy Fair in 2001, and I hadn't decided what industry I wanted to get back into. It would either be the toy industry or the TV Industry. It was in the aftermath of 9/11 and jobs were scarce.

I decided to visit an old studio merchandising associate to see if he could use my marketing help. He wanted me on board but couldn't quite afford the salary I needed to keep my family supported. I hit upon the idea of working part-time for him, allowing me to do my own thing and design my next entrepreneurial business or project with the time I wasn't on the clock with him.

Thus, the beginning of my own "montage" was born. I only see it in hindsight, of course, but for you, it can be planned and executed in advance.

MANY PIECES CAN MAKE UP THE WHOLE

Author and speaker Julie Shifman coined the term "Portfolio Career" to describe the concept of multiple, simultaneous revenue streams to make a living. Julie's book *Act Three* is a great one to check out and provides a more detailed explanation of this concept.

I call my version of this idea a "Montage Career" since I come at things from a more visual and creative angle. The Oxford English Dictionary defines montage as "The process or technique of selecting, editing, and piecing together separate sections of film to create a continuous whole."

The idea of "wholeness" in life has always been attractive to me. However, I'm also realistic and realize it doesn't necessarily just come one day and stay forever; life happens and things constantly change. But as you start this process of nurturing your more creative self, it makes sense to plan and at least try to design as much wholeness and balance as you can. Like we did with the life roles exercise in Chapter 3, this can be a blend of a better montage for you going forward. It is also the beginning of a roadmap to help you take actions that will actualize your Creative YOU Turn life.

In an article about portfolio careers on PBS's *Next Avenue*, Julie Shifman also says this type of career is "ideal for people who can answer 'true' to one or more of the following statements:

1. You get bored easily doing the same type of job over and over.
2. You either need or prefer a flexible work schedule.
3. You'd like to have or need the multiple income streams that a portfolio career can provide."

In an interview with her I found out Julie has had a portfolio career herself and says she falls into the first category of getting bored easily. Her "portfolio" includes running a career advisory business, coaching clients, writing books, managing real estate, teaching at a university, and delivering speeches to women's groups. She also serves on the boards of several nonprofit organizations and creates inspirational events for women. Oh, and if that isn't enough, in her spare time she teaches ballet.

Feeling overwhelmed? It can often feel that way when we are confronted with doers and achievers, but the trick to setting the life you want in motion and making things happen is to simply start. Once you take any action whatsoever, other actions will appear or fall into place, then others, and before you know it, by steadily taking small actions each day, you'll suddenly be giving people like Julie a run for their money.

The next section of this chapter is really the heart and soul of my Creative YOU Turn program. It imagines a plan where you are able to build and execute this Montage Career in advance rather than seeing it from the rearview mirror like I did. In other words, be purposeful and proactive rather than reactive.

It's no secret that since the downturn of 2008, and more recently the Covid-19 pandemic of 2020, there has been a stark reduction in jobs that offer pensions or retirement security. Even with the economy's recovery, the idea that career security will return is unlikely. My hunch, and a reflection of my own experience, is this is a trend that will continue as the U.S. population ages. Everything from potential jobs, employers unwilling to pay benefits, Social Security income – all the things that might create a Montage Career for people of a certain age – will become more attractive and necessary.

Having found themselves laid off during the pandemic and struggling to find anything close to full-time employment, many people learned they could have part-time jobs and create multiple streams of income to supplement those jobs (the "montage"). At a certain point in life, you may also find you have multiple equally developed skills sets. My own career had been divided evenly between the television industry, theme parks, and toys and merchandising. Now, I'm doing on-air TV work and career coaching. My skills from all of these areas provide me with a living and constitute my Montage Career.

MUTIPLE SKILLS CAN MEAN MULTIPLE REVENUE STREAMS

Having multiple jobs in multiple industries might be the best thing that happened to you. Even if you've been in the same job for 25 years, I'm sure you've delved into many interests along the way, and a broad skill set only increases your earning potential. Think about it… What do Leonardo da Vinci, actress Hedy Lamarr, Brian May of the rock group Queen and Mr. Rogers all have in common? They can all be referred to as "Renaissance people" because they are accomplished in multiple areas of their lives and careers.

Leonardo da Vinci, with all of his many accomplishments in art and science, was the original source for the phrase "Renaissance man". Brian May, the lead guitarist of the rock group Queen, has a PhD in astrophysics and is a university chancellor. He also has an asteroid named after him and got his PhD in astrophysics after a hiatus of 37 years! Hedy Lamarr, a Hollywood beauty and leading lady, invented the gyroscopic technology on torpedoes that helped win World War II (her invention is one of the main components used in cellphone technology today). And in addition to being a host for his famous show *Mister Rogers' Neighborhood*, Fred Rogers was also an ordained Presbyterian minister and a very accomplished musician, having written over two hundred songs, including children's operas and the theme song for his television show.

  ˙ Yet from another perspective, you could also say about all of them (and I'm sure many of their friends and families did!) "Geez, can't you stick with anything?! You're all over the place – Jack of all trades, master of none!" Sound familiar?

We don't say that about these people, however, because in hindsight and with some historical perspective, they had great success in multiple areas and somehow managed to make a living (we assume) out of their various endeavors. You can imagine it was a much different scenario during their journey and while they were working. Naysayers and their own self-doubts surely abounded. Any review of Da Vinci's life or sketchbooks would also show many unfinished projects and shiny objects pursued at the expense of more practical and financially beneficial endeavors.

HAPPY TOGETHER – A TALE OF TWO TURTLES

One of my favorite examples of being open to a new life and finding a Montage Career is my good friend and former business partner Mark Volman. Mark was a founding member of the 1960's Top 40 rock group The Turtles. Their famous hit song, "Happy Together," has probably been in more movies and commercials than any other piece of music from that era.

There's no category I can think of that's more set in stone than "60's Rock Star". How do you wiggle out of that one and have a Career YOU Turn to find your next chapter? And, furthermore, why? In Mark's case, all it took was a bike ride.

Growing up in Torrance, California, in the same city as the Beach Boys, he and Howard Kaylan, a classmate, had an incredible ability to harmonize. When Mark was eighteen, they launched The Turtles and had their first hit record. Unfortunately, he had to stay home during their first tour because he was still in high school!

Mark's evolutionary career is quite profound. The Turtles had a number of hit songs, including "Happy Together" and "Elenore".

They achieved great success. But, like all great bands, there came a point when they decided to call it quits. After they disbanded, Mark and Howard Kaylan joined Frank Zappa and The Mothers of Invention as The Phlorescent Leech & Eddie (which became Flo and Eddie), where they performed vocals with stars like John Lennon, Sammy Hagar, Hoyt Axton, and Duran Duran, as well as a hit drive time radio show.

During an interview, I asked him what a peak moment in his life was, and he said it was being a kid from Torrance, California, singing in front of American royalty at Tricia Nixon's wedding at the White House.

He also worked on sixteen children's music albums while he was in his early thirties, wrote music scores for films, and managed to turn his time during and post-Turtles into a pretty substantial living.

One day, as Mark was riding his bicycle past L.A. City College, he decided to stop in to see what it would take to get a degree since he had never gone to college. Soon thereafter, he entered a program that led to a Bachelor's degree and then received a Master of Fine Arts degree with an emphasis in Film Studies and Screenwriting from Loyola Marymount University. So much for the rock star stereotype!

He's currently an Associate Professor and Coordinator of the Entertainment Industry Studies Program at Belmont University in the Mike Curb College of Entertainment and Music Business in Nashville, Tennessee. A fun guy by nature, Mark talked about his exciting life with The Turtles during our conversation. He also talked about how he knew higher education could play a role in getting him into a different career. When he realized he didn't have to live off being a 60's rock star, he segued into academics and is still having a great time.

To do that, he joined a "support tribe" by going back to school. He emphatically said he could not have done it on his own. He needed the training and credentials to get his new career up and running. Now, he has the ultimate Montage Career – touring during the summer months, getting income from Turtles merchandise and records, and being a college professor the rest of the time. Not bad!

As you start shaping your Montage Career, you'll need some sort of steady paycheck to get started, unless you've already retired or have a primary source of income and you're looking to expand a secondary or side gig.

For most of us, it's just too hard to get things off the ground without some sort of security. This is when you have to look around you and get creative. Many opportunities are right in front of us. You may already have something we actors call our day job, or our primary source of income, while we go out on auditions. Although the part-time job can often feel like it gets in the way of pursuing the true freedom you are seeking in your Creative YOU Turn, think of it more as the sustainable baseline you need to experiment with your other potential selves.

For me, this has varied from corporate gigs to designing my last business, that I sold and was able to run for the new owners on a flexible at-home basis. This has allowed me to subsidize my other Creative YOU Turn experiments over the last ten years.

In her article "How to Create a Career Without a Full-Time Job" published in *U.S. News and World Report*, Alexis Grant emphasizes the idea of having a part-time job as a launching pad for a portfolio career, rather than trying to create something out of whole cloth:

"Consider finding a steady part-time gig that you can depend on. This is especially important in the beginning, and it's how many slashers [a phrase she uses for people who have portfolio careers] get their start. Having money you can count on goes a long way toward helping you feel comfortable without a full-time paycheck."

One of my coaching clients has three "jobs" at the same time: Two days per week she works on-site for a nonprofit organization to help sell sponsorships, and she also works for two large clients as a freelance advertising salesperson. This flexible schedule allows her to devote time to exploring real estate investments with her partner and to her own charity for underprivileged seniors who can't afford food for their pets. I know it sounds like my client has a great deal on her plate, but she manages to pull it off because she's motivated and driven to make it all work. Having a payoff goal like her non-profit makes it all worthwhile. As you start adding more actions and identities to your life, you'll often find that the more you do, the more you can do.

CREATING YOUR UNIQUE MONTAGE

How do you determine the best course for your Montage Career? Until age 55, because I was self-employed a good deal of the time, I learned how to seek clients and customers for my various marketing companies. I'd listen intently and proactively to their goals and concerns. In essence, my jobs were created from listening to clients' needs.

The ability to identify and create opportunities for myself based on client needs, combined with my background in television, entertainment marketing and merchandising, established a skill set over the years that allowed me the Montage Career I'm enjoying today. Part of determining your dream Montage Career is to assess your skills and then find the threads you can weave together in your goals and activities. These, in turn, will provide the jobs to create the full-time income and creative experience you want.

Another great article, "8 Tips for Managing a Portfolio Career" by Hester Lacey in *Forbes*, quotes an interview she did with Fred Deakins, who specializes in interactive art projects. He is a professor of Interactive Design at the University of Arts in London and is a prime example of someone who designed their own career. One of Fred's suggestions I like most is to "fly many missions," which means you should research and do many projects, then see which one makes the most sense for your career path. By doing this, you can get a more effective sense of something you could for 10, 20 or 30 hours a week – but which you might not want to do 40 hours a week.

When I started my acting career, I thought I wanted to work in television and film and also to be on stage. When I had the opportunity to have my own television show on career transitions, I quickly realized I preferred doing interviews and being a talk show host, so I let acting go by the wayside. However, if I hadn't gone into acting and then commercial work, I wouldn't have received the experience that made me a capable television talk show host. So, "flying many missions" is a great example of how one thing leads to another, and you can eventually find your true calling in an arena that fits you perfectly.

Another of Hester's eight tips is to be "selective and organized," since it's very easy to become distracted while trying to create a multi-thread Montage Career. Echoing Hester, Fred Deakins also says you have to learn how to say no and be selective: "I have about three ideas for books, but I need to be sure one of them is great before taking it on. I have a definitive cycle where I switch from planning, pitching and proposing into creating. When you're working it has to be immersive: at that point, the shutters go down." The job at one of Fred's corporate clients is a very unconventional part-time position. He told them, "For those two months I'm yours, but the rest of the time don't even email me. I'm much better at saying no these days. I used to say yes to everything."

I have many false starts and unfinished projects on my plate, but I think that's true for anyone who's in the midst of a career transition. While determining the direction of your Montage Career, you need to be aware of what you can realistically achieve (which you might be already doing). In my case, it was my part-time entertainment marketing job, which segued into having a flexible job with the company I owned and eventually sold (Incentive Plus Network). I was then able to combine that job with my teaching, coaching and having my own television show. Talk about a win/win!

HOBBIES CAN BE THE ANSWER FOR ADDITIONAL MONTAGE REVENUE

One of my favorite books about making a Creative YOU Turn is Nancy Collamer's *Second Act Careers: 50+ Ways to Profit from Your Passions in Semi-Retirement*. Although Nancy doesn't mention creative careers in too much detail, she did write an article I love about making hobbies pay. Since I can't imagine improving on Nancy's list, with her permission I'm including it here at length:

"Continuing to work in retirement isn't all that uncommon. A 2017 report conducted by the Transamerica Center for Retirement Studies found that fifty-three percent of U.S. workers expect to retire after sixty-five or don't plan to retire, while fifty-six percent intend to take on part-time work.

Instead of picking up random jobs to fill your days, consider turning your hobby into a business or finding work in your field of interest. You'll make a little money to pad your savings while practicing your passion.

Teach What You Love

Whether you're a skilled photographer, chef or engineer, chances are you can find work teaching what you love. You can set up shop in your home – like your neighborhood piano teacher – or teach at a local adult education program or school.

Alternatively, you can become an instructor for online instructional platforms like Udemy. But, if you prefer face-to-face interaction, Craigslist is a good place to find tutoring work.

If you have a knack for editing video, YouTube is a great place for you to post instructional videos, product reviews and more. Although you won't make a ton of money at first, successful YouTubers can rack in quite a bit off ads shown on their videos.

Sell Your Products Online

In the past, crafty individuals only had the opportunity to sell handmade goods at fairs and farmers markets. But thanks to the proliferation of online marketplaces, you can now sell your creations worldwide.

Etsy is the best-known marketplace for artisans, but there are plenty of smaller sites you can consider, like ArtFire and Zibbet. You can also use eBay to sell your creations. Even if you don't make a lot of money, you can file a tax deduction for your hobby to help offset costs.

A lot of online craftspeople make shirts, posters and knickknacks for trendy TV shows like *Game of Thrones* and *Doctor Who*. These shows have large audiences that are looking for unique items they can display or wear.

Write About Your Experiences or Crafts

Whether you carve out wood sculptures or explore hiking trails in your city, chances are you can find people online interested in what you do.

Start your own blog and post photos of your creations, favorite trails or foods you cook. If you enjoy writing, create a DIY blog that provides step-by-step instructions with photos. You can even post your work to Instagram or BuzzFeed, which might help boost sales or viewership.

If you don't want to bank on ad revenue and sponsorships for income, pick up freelance writing assignments on sites like Mediabistro and FlexJobs.

Create Products for Your Hobby

Yoga enthusiasts need mats; cooks need knives; and gym rats need fitness journals. If you can invent a product that fills a gap in your field of interest, you can make quite a bit of money.

As an enthusiast, think about products that would make enjoying your hobby safer or more efficient. You can even make pins and bumper stickers so other enthusiasts can share their love for a hobby. If you're not sure whether there's a market for something you have in mind, make a prototype for yourself and share it online to gauge interest. You might be surprised by the reception and find yourself starting a small business.

Lead a Tour

Americans are on the move. In 2016, they made 1.7 billion trips for leisure, according to the most recent data from the U.S. Travel Association. That amounts to $683.1 billion in travel spending for the year. With so many travelers on the move, you can easily set up and run bird-watching groups, brewery tours or bike tours, where you lead tourists to attractions around the city.

The company Cheese Journeys, for example, offers a behind-the-scenes look at how cheese and wine is made. Tourists can sign up for tours to meet culinary experts and get hands-on experience in a new city. Some of these ideas like on-site tours have changed post- Covid of course, but virtual tours have taken their place and variations will exist going forward.

Find Part-Time Work

From the baseball fan who writes about spring training for his local paper to the movie enthusiast who works as an usher at the local arts center, finding a job related to your hobby is a wonderful way to blend work and fun. Think about the places you like to spend your free time – ballparks, bookstores, gardening centers – and see if they have any part-time openings.

You can even find seasonal work for resorts, national parks and tourist attractions. CoolWorks.com has job openings for tour guides, community managers and guest services at resorts, letting you enjoy the outdoors, meet new people or just have a picturesque workplace to enjoy your golden years

Rent Out Your Space

Do you like meeting new people and have extra space in your home? You can rent out rooms to travelers. This could be one of the best money-making hobbies for retirees who live in big cities or near popular vacation destinations.

Think about that extra room in your house, basement or even garage and how it can be used to accommodate vacationers. Once you consider how you can use the space, you can then pick the platform to advertise and promote your place of residence. There are many options, including Airbnb, Flipkey and Vrbo.

Become a Consultant

What sets a retiree apart from everyone else? A lifetime of experience. One of the most lucrative hobbies for a retiree is becoming a professional consultant. You can work as a consultant in your professional area or become a consultant in a hobby that you like and are good at. For example, maybe you're a great gardener and received "yard of the month" more than once in the neighborhood. Advise others how they too can get a garden like yours.

For more of this great info, visit Nancy's website: www. mylifestylecareer.com.

BE TRANSPARENT ABOUT YOUR GOAL

Nancy's list is very inspirational but it can still be a struggle to get started. One thing I think is very difficult for many people going into a

Montage Career in terms of ego and prestige is answering the question, "What do you do for a living?" and having to say (in my case), "I'm a TV marketing executive/commercial actor/print model/TV talk show host/author." Who can spit that out all at once, let alone fit it all onto a business card?

The more you're transparent with people about your goal of having a Montage Career, the more helpful they and the universe will be in helping you achieve your goal. You might find the people at your part-time job will understand what you're wanting to achieve (probably because many have the same aspirations), and they might even provide ways to help you achieve your goal. For example, when my part-time employer C&S Sales became one of my strategic partners for Incentive Plus Network, I shared what I was doing and they saw the value in it for them.

Another avenue many people are taking is hiring a career coach who has experience transitioning people into a new career. One aspect of my own "montage" is being a career coach, and many authors and specialists in certain fields have found that a calling as well.

Here's one way to determine how many pieces of creative capital it will take to make your Montage Career work. This is whether it's full-time employment, part-time supplement or simply a self-sustaining hobby.

MONTAGE CAREER WORKSHEET

1. How much do I need to live on and save each month/year? (See budget resources below.) _____

2. What are my fixed expenses and how much (e.g. mortgage, insurance, etc.)
   _____

3. What are my "rough" optional expenses and how much month/year? (cable TV, vacations, etc.)
   _____

4. Where do I get most of my income from now (Primary job, pension, Soc. Sec, etc.) How much?
   _____

5. What are some secondary income streams (rentals, freelance work, garage sales, stocks, etc.?) How much? Month/Year?
   _____

6. What career experiments/action that I'm doing that can create income (e.g. rental, freelance, sell assets)
   _____

7. What proportion can I grow #6 within 2 years?
   _____

8. What can I adjust in #1, 2 & 3 to equal #7?
   _____

9. What are the hobbies or skills I can use immediately to be the "core" income for my Montage Career
   _____

10. Explore the following budget apps and choose the one that works best for you: https://www.nerdwallet.com/blog/finance/budgeting-saving-tools/ (I personally recommend Mint or You Need a Budget.)

CHAPTER 7

Magical People & Action Partners

"A mentor is someone who allows you to see the
hope inside yourself." — Oprah Winfrey

CREATING YOUR NEW CREATIVE NETWORK

RECENTLY I GOT THE SCULPTING bug again. I had done some
sculpting in high school but had never pursued it seriously. I worked
with many sculptors during my years in the toy industry and always
marveled at their skills, and once I finally put my desire "out there",
a person showed up in a men's support group I attend that happens to
be a very successful Hollywood special effects sculptor. I asked him if
he knew of any sculpting classes I could attend or private instructors I
could hire. His response was "How about me?" I knew I could never
afford him, but before I even asked about a cost he said, "You get the
supplies and I'll do it for free." I was flabbergasted. We've been doing
a weekly session ever since then.

I now get to take joyful "sculpting breaks" during my day. In my
Creative YOU Turn space there is a dedicated place for my sculpting.
It has my current project (a bust of Jack Nicholson) as well as tools and
reference pics. At times, especially when I'm in need of a change from
work tasks, I can pick up Jack and feel the therapeutic fun of the clay in
my fingers and the sense of wonder at the structure of the human face.

None of this existed six months ago. Getting back to sculpting is something I've "thought" about for 20+ years but once I put it out there and said it aloud, once I named it, my magic person appeared and off I went!

What magic person is waiting in the wings for you? Once you ask or at least start to make your dreams and aspirations known in an appropriate way, they DO appear. Trust me.

I mentioned in an earlier chapter how I "magically" got a job at a local television station in Los Angeles pretty much based on serendipity and being at the right place at the right time. A salesman at KTTV connected me with the head of Creative Services who saw something about me that he needed in his department (even though I had no previous television experience). The fact that he took me on in good faith can only be deemed as magical.

It was the beginning of a long career in television, which might not have happened if I hadn't gone to the workshop at the station where I met the salesman. Otherwise, I might have returned to school, or taken other avenues.

One of the key elements of creating your YOU Turn plan is tapping into a new network or support group of people. If you have an established career or network of associates, this may sound counterintuitive. Surely it's these people that know you best and can help you along your new path. That may be true for certain areas like getting your part-time "foundation" job, but to really start succeeding in your new creative areas you'll likely want to build and nurture a new network of people. This is where the concept of "magic people" comes in. This is a phrase the sculptor Robert Tolone used in one of my show interviews, and it continues to resonate with me.

Through my interviews with Robert and other creatives on my show *Remade in America*, I've noticed that many of them have had magical avatars that seem to drop down out of the heavens. They open the door to a new career by making a phone call to get them into a company, job, play, television show or an art gallery, and from there great things happen.

Again, they don't have to be superstar, major league accomplishments. But sometimes all it takes is just the right twist of fate to make somebody aware they can earn a living doing their passion, or at least give them access to something that's close to their passion.

Magical people can appear out of nowhere. Maybe they arrive in a situation where a particular skill is the link to a career advancement or in the guise of somebody who will nudge you along. Whatever the case may, when a magical person shows up you need to pay attention because great things are bound to happen! Often they are teachers in our new areas or simply people we find that do what we are wanting to do. The key with "magical people" is to be honest and direct with what you are hoping they can help you achieve.

A Few Famous Magical People

I read a lot of biographies, and the main thing I've learned from the biographies of successful people, particularly politician and performers, is that most had a mentor to help guide them to success. Often it was an engaged or successful parent (Kirk and Michael Douglas, Henry and Jane Fonda, John Adams and John Quincy Adams, George H.W. Bush and George W. Bush, et al.). Most of us, however, who don't have the privilege of being born into a famous family, have to find our mentors and magical people in the creative universe about us. Here a few examples of how that has happened:

1. Oprah Winfrey had Maya Angelou
2. Mark Zuckerberg had Steve Jobs
3. Bill Gates had Warren Buffet
4. Elizabeth Taylor had Audrey Hepburn
5. Steven Spielberg had Universal President Lew Wasserman

Now, think of who **you** might have.

Being Magical for Others

During my interview with artist and sculptor Robert Tolone, he kindly mentioned *me* as a magical person (which is where I got that phrase). While I was in the toy industry doing a job for *Snow White and the Seven Dwarfs*, I asked him if he could sculpt the seven individual figures for me, and without hesitation he said "Sure!" (I found out later it was the first time he had ever sculpted a cartoon character, let alone one that had to pass the rigorous muster of the Disney Studios character integrity department.)

Much like people at KTTV appreciating my skills, I very much appreciated Robert and his many talents which landed him a career-changing assignment. So, in essence, I guess I was his magical person who gave him a golden opportunity because he was in the right place at the right time and he did the right thing.

I believe when we give back to the universe that has given to us, we keep those powers of magic alive in our lives. Think of it as an unspoken contract you make with the world – if people are magical for me, then I will be magical for others. In this way, we can create a new belief and faith in the unexpected miracles that might present themselves at any moment in our lives, but we are also telling the universe and the people in it that we are generous with our gifts, knowledge, and resources, and in giving freely of ourselves we keep the power of magic alive not only for the person we're helping in the moment, but for the numerous people that person might help in turn, on and on down the line.

Your Creative YOU Turn Partner-accountability

A CYT Partner is going to be a primary asset in terms of simplifying your plan and keeping you on track. You don't need to meet with them in person (unless you want to). You can ZOOM or Skype them, email them a PowerPoint page or a photo of your brand board, or go over it with them on the phone. The main thing is not to procrastinate or come up with reasons why you don't want to do it, because it's an invaluable tool to help you make a good living for the rest of your life.

Your CYT partner can be a mentor, a coach, a friend, or whoever comes to mind that has the time. They probably shouldn't be your spouse/partner or family member. Choose someone who will make you feel safe and supported and who has an objective point-of-view.

The premise of my book is how to reinvent and transform yourself in a more informative and focused fashion. Arthur Miller, the famous American playwright, once said the problem with a creative person being a business person is that they see potential in everything. So when working with people as a personal and business coach, one of the attributes I bring to the table is how to focus people and help them eliminate unnecessary steps to get them to their goal.

My own coach, Bob Dickman, helps me stay on track as I have a creative mind that's all over the place. I write words in big letters on pieces of paper and put them on giant pieces of foam core or Post-it easels, then hang or tape them to a wall. These visual cues ground me throughout the workday but also in passing, so those big, specific words seep into my subconscious mind all the time, keeping me on track and centered on what I initially set out to accomplish.

A Magical Person "Bank Shot"

I previously mentioned my interview with Stan Freese, who told the story of being a high school music teacher in Minneapolis when he was asked to play the tuba in Russia. Even though the opportunity had come via the school, he was afraid he'd be frowned on by taking time off to do something he considered frivolous.

After he turned the gig down, the State Department called the school and said, "Mr. Freese is *strongly* urged to take this opportunity." Or, as Stan colorfully puts it, "The fat boy *is* going to Russia!"

Of course, this isn't an example of a magical person who propelled Stan's career into a new direction; it was just someone at the State Department who probably had promised the program to somebody high up and didn't want borscht on his face. But this was a crowning moment in his career that taught him the power of taking every opportunity as it presents itself.

After Stan played in Russia, he was asked to play at the White House for President Nixon, Secretary of State Henry Kissinger, and Soviet Ambassador Anatoly Dobrynin. As Stan tells it, it was a "slow news day." Because of remarks Kissinger and Dobrynin had made about his notes sounding better than what they were doing, he ended up on the front page of *The New York Times* standing beside President Nixon.

Stan's newsworthy appearance then came to the attention of people putting the finishing touches on Walt Disney World down in Orlando, Florida (are you seeing the domino effect?). They needed musicians for their marching band, so they called Stan to audition as a tuba player.

However, because he had played gigs in high school and college, had been an emcee, had a great Midwest vibe about him, and was very comfortable performing in front of people, they instead asked him to be the leader of the Disneyland band, and thus began his 42-year career.

Everyone I interview has incredible amounts of talent, but sometimes talent isn't enough. There are plenty of talented, capable people in the world, but some simply have a knack for...

Doing the Right Thing in the Right Place at the Right Time

This chapter on magical people is also about preparing yourself for how to act when they show up in your life. To be able to hear their knock on the door and to be rested enough to run the race into a whole new stadium of opportunities can be a difficult thing to do. It can be particularly difficult after having a career that had its ups and downs and maybe some incredible early successes, and then petered out into a bit of a drudge or just doing it for the paycheck.

It's important not to apply that "realistic cynic" to this new creative pursuit. Be naïve! Be a newcomer! Be a neophyte! You truly don't know this path. And that's the fun of it. Absolutely anything can happen, so stay open.

One of the goals I have for my coaching clients is to foster in them the ability to act quickly when magical people or situations show up.

Don't Just Do Something... Sit There!

Rule number one in getting ready for magical people to arrive in your life is to relax. Pause and take a "life breath". If you don't have enough money – and your job prevents your house from being repossessed – the timing might not be right. However, for people who are making CYT decisions the tendency is to take action, action, action!

I love the phrase "we are human beings – not human doings." Sometimes the goal is to just be, so doing something repetitively that's not properly focused (even though it feels constructive and powerful), can in fact be counterproductive.

In my own career, there have been instances where I pushed too hard and ended up in places I shouldn't have been in career-wise. There have also been projects that I kept persisting in, despite many red flags, and that probably should have died a natural death long before I realized it. These mistakes can be expensive in time and in treasure.

A primary focus of my Business of Art class was how to prepare a creative portfolio, website, or presentation that would create enough interest to land a full-time job, or help bring in clients for a new creative business.

Every semester I was shocked to hear how my students were applying for jobs. Most would say, "I emailed twenty resumes today." Or, "I posted something on jobs.com." Or, "I did this or that digital thing." It makes sense that's how they'd perceive today's world of applying for a job, because most large corporations insist people submit their applications digitally: "Please do not contact us directly. Fill out this form and submit via xyz." Even my own Gen-X and Millennial daughters were sending out tons of resumes via the Internet with little to no response.

So I had Esther Glumace, the head of H.R. for Toshiba in Orange County, speak to my primarily twenty-something students about applying for and getting jobs. At that time, only a small percentage of Toshiba's hiring came from online submissions, and the vast majority of new hires were references from existing employees. In fact, they incentivized employees to find people for them to save them the headache of sifting through thousands of applicants.

Why would this be a good way to hire new employees? You immediately have a reference for someone you know and trust, or maybe you'd know *not* to hire somebody depending on who referred them. So in this case, connections within a certain industry – whether it be high-tech or entertainment – were always referrals or "word-of-mouth".

One of the main goals for anyone getting into a new creative career or trying to find a new job is to be in a place where they can create good word-of-mouth about themselves. If many jobs are obtained via referrals, how can you utilize this to your advantage?

You may be thinking, *but these examples you gave are from a while ago. What about now?* Since the world changes quickly and dramatically, and nearly everything is digital, do old stories apply to today's remade environment? I think that's a valid question, and the truth probably lies somewhere in between.

I have all the social media tools imaginable at my fingertips, and some of them are quite effective for very specific tasks. The main thing I know about all of the great digital tools out there is that they primarily create awareness, but it's still VERY important to be able to turn that awareness into an interview that either lands you a job or gets you a client for your new creative endeavor.

Fake It 'Til You Make It

Jason Freese – the keyboardist for the hugely successful band Green Day – has a similar story to his dad Stan's. He talks about taking a $100 gig with a punk band where he met a techie for the Eagles who told him Joe Walsh was auditioning keyboard players proficient on the Hammond B3 (a difficult type of instrument with a very unique sound).

Unsure if he could master the keyboard, Jason agreed to audition because his dad had told him to take any gig while growing his career. He played a song he didn't think was Joe's style of music, and Walsh hired him on the spot because he liked Jason's energy as well as his technical proficiency.

This career juggernaut eventually led him to play with the Goo Goo Dolls, and then with Green Day, who he's toured the world with for the past ten years. So Jason's magical person was the techie in the punk band who led him to a gig he really didn't want to do. By saying "yes," he launched a career with an entirely new instrument that's carried him until this day.

Be Ready When Your Magic Opportunity Knocks

Jason and Stan Freese are ardent, devoted musicians, and they've both said the biggest part of their success was that they practiced four or five hours per day. They were prepared, so when the call came for Stan to go to Russia and for Jason to play the Hammond B3 for Joe Walsh, they were already proficient musicians. Then they used those opportunities to take them to their next steps in their careers.

You'll need to have a solid portfolio that's above and beyond a resume. Everyone has a story to tell, so think of your career portfolio as a montage of real-life stories about why you did certain things and the successes you've had beyond "I sold X amount of this art" or "I've played here or there".

I have a good friend who interviewed for a nursing job at a very prestigious hospital. She'd been going through some personal challenges and was leery about sharing that information with her potential employer. But, as she sat before a panel of interviewers, she bravely revealed her story, and how she faced her challenges, which she felt showed her to be flexible, resilient, and devoted to her career. She ended up getting one of two openings out of 90 applications.

When I've interviewed people for jobs, particularly when I was at Disney, it was always people's personality that determined who I wanted to work with and who would fit in well with the team. So rehearse, rehearse, and rehearse in terms of your own ability to discuss your most vibrant and valuable product: YOU! Start by being your own magical person and then go forth from there.

1. Who are some "magical people" I might connect with? (List at least 5)

_____

_____

_____

_____

2. How can I contact them and when will I? (Be specific: LinkedIn, email, phone, etc.)

_____

_____

_____

_____

3. Who might be my accountability buddy? (List at least 3)

_____

_____

_____

_____

4. What are the 3 primary things I can be accountable to them first about (Be specific: job search, creative space diagram, etc.)

_____

_____

_____

_____

CHAPTER 8

Order, Focus & The Next Indicated Thing

"The lure of the distant and the difficult is deceptive. The great opportunity is where you are." — John Burroughs

Pay MORE Attention to that Man Behind the Curtain

YOU MAY KNOW THE SCENE in the classic movie, *The Wizard of Oz*, where Dorothy and her companions are facing the giant image of the Wizard. While he's admonishing them and smoke bombs are going off, Toto scurries over to an area off to the side and pulls the curtain back to expose an old man pulling levers and yelling into a microphone.

When the man turns around to see them staring at him, he shouts into the microphone, "Pay no attention to that man behind the curtain!", which is when the audience realizes the powerful voice of the Wizard of Oz was really coming from the old man.

I used to use that scene as a metaphor to describe marketing and promotion as the guy "behind the curtain" who could create an image much greater than the reality. But as time progressed, I now see it as a different type of metaphor for my own journey of self-discovery.

Just think about the many wonderful things that were put into play after the "crisis" of being discovered by Toto. Being exposed allowed the Wizard to quit pretending to be a magical being and instead just be himself while teaching Dorothy, the Lion, the Tin Man, and the Scarecrow invaluable lessons.

The freedom of discovery allowed him to achieve his ultimate goal of getting into his hot air balloon and returning home to Kansas. If it hadn't been for Toto pulling that curtain back, he probably would have stayed in Oz and pulled those levers for the rest of his empty, lonely life. This "controlled discovery" also had a ripple effect of freeing the people of Oz from the same "pretend" source of protection, so everyone around him benefitted from his being discovered.

Over the years, you've probably built images and created smoke screens and amplifications that obscured the truth of who you really are. The "coming out" to be yourself can be a very liberating and life-altering process. So how do you discover that true person behind the curtain? How do you peel back the layers to find the successful and contented person you know you can become?

Success is Subtraction, Not Addition

This whole creative transition process is a hard and at times very taxing thing to do! If it was easy, you wouldn't need this book. So part of setting yourself up for success is to take care of the WHOLE artist that is you. Living your life as you truly are and where you truly are right now. Not some perfect time in the future when you're living in the perfect city with the perfect partner and the perfect house or once you've lost 15 pounds. But right now! As you are.

Decide right away in this Creative YOU Turn process that it isn't worth doing this unless you maintain your physical, emotional, and spiritual health. As important as all the time spent in your art and creative process is, please do yourself the favor of allowing time for exercise, healthy food, having fun in non-self-improvement activities, and some form of spiritual practice. When I say spiritual, I use that in the broadest sense of whatever makes you feel you are a part of and connected to the universe and the rest of humanity. Whether that's church time, meditation, surfing or something else, only you know what does that for you. Make it a part of this plan and factor it in as you would practicing your instrument, writing or performing.

De-clutter Your Gutter

One of the biggest impediments to remaking yourself is clutter and distractions, so I think the process needs to begin with decluttering. I'm not talking about physical clutter (though that can be distracting), I'm talking about mental clutter and how it can limit your ability to take action.

I had an urge to perform and be on stage at a very young age, so I did puppet shows and ventriloquism and magic acts. Somewhere along the line, I became self-conscious and put all those things aside, and decided it was much easier to be behind the curtain and supporting people who were in the limelight. I've had a wonderful career doing that, and I don't regret one minute of it.

However, while I was in the midst of analyzing my career transition, I found that some of the clutter, limitations, and prerequisites of what I could and couldn't do had been squeezed out of me, though not necessarily in a negative way. My business had been successful, and my partner and I were getting ready to sell it to a large advertising agency.

But in terms of what I was willing and able to do, the blinders I had been wearing were removed to help me see my life more lucidly. There were changes ahead, but it wasn't clear as to what they would be.

Controlled Discovery & Being Reawakened

A favorite spiritual author, Emmett Fox, has a unique take on the concept of the "second coming" of Christ. He believes that rather than an actual physical manifestation, it's simply a reawakening of God-consciousness, or the "Christ" within people. No matter your faith (or lack of one), this idea of reawakening to your true self in order to live your dream is profound and not to be missed.

I often reflect on magical spiritual moments I've had, like a time when I was a young boy looking up into the eucalyptus trees walking to school and a stillness and calm came upon me and I felt a profound oneness with the world. A bookend experience was during a trip to Philadelphia where I created a six-foot tall Mickey Mouse display for the opening of Paris Disneyland for travel agencies all over the world.

I had some time to kill while the manufacturer and technical staff were working on details for my project. When I travel on business I always go to art museums, so I found myself wandering into the Philadelphia Museum of Art (famous for its *Rocky* sequence on the steps with Sylvester Stallone), which surprisingly is also where the permanent collection of one of my favorite artists, Marcel Duchamp, is still on display. What a treat that was!

Duchamp was a game-changer in the art world who unfortunately is remembered for his urinal fountain and some of the coarser aspects of what he created. But to me he will always be one of the more cerebral and clever artists who invented the "ready-mades," which is setting an everyday item like a wine rack or a bicycle wheel in a different environment, putting a spotlight on it, and saying "this is art." This style of artistic expression that's taken for granted now was not appreciated back in the early 20th century when Duchamp was part of the European avant-garde Dadaist movement.

I sauntered through the museum and saw many of his amazing pieces. When I finished, I then ended up in the bookstore where I thumbed through a book about one of Duchamp's pieces called *Étant donnés* (Given: 1. The Waterfall, 2. The Illuminating Gas). It's composed of a battered wood door through which one views a landscape of trees and a waterfall, and a nude woman lying down holding a gas lamp. It was his last piece and was worked on in secret for many years only to be put on public display after his death in 1967.

When I realized I hadn't seen this piece upstairs, I asked the book clerk where it was, and she told me it was on display in an area I obviously missed during my walk-through. I returned to the Duchamp area, and lo and behold, over in the corner was an entranceway to another room I had assumed was for another artist. I walked in and was met by a large wooden door that had two small holes at about eye level through which I could see a bit of light.

I looked through the holes and saw a tableau I can only describe as "controlled discovery." (The artist creates a space he wants the visitor to happen upon by accident. But once he has their attention, he is in total control of what he wants them to see.)

I almost missed Duchamp's most important piece. It was hidden from me as I went through and saw the familiar pieces that I knew and didn't know to look for the "secret" piece.

This idea of finding your true "secret" self behind the "curtain" where you've been hiding, and balancing it with the other aspects of your life, is important. By extension, sharing aspects of this idea with other areas of your life like your career is fundamental in developing your Montage Career.

Remaking myself and allowing myself to have new dreams, aspirations, and possibilities has always been predicated on my willingness to take action. There are certain moments I need to pay attention to where I feel total unity and contentment, and in my professional life those moments usually occur around art and the creative process. In my personal life, it is around my children, family, and often when helping a coaching client. It's the moment when I feel flow, being in the zone, or simply getting goosebumps. They are few and far between at first, but I have learned to pay close attention to them and even started to expect them. It now happens regularly in the middle of a coaching session with a client where I can feel the "flow" of being of service and the client responding to some input. It gives me goosebumps. Your new career should give you goosebumps, too!

It can also be in what I'm sketching or painting, or when I'm playing the drums, and it's been happening more and more in my acting career. It's likely a direct result of doing my *Best of California* television show that combines so many of my passions. But when I look back on my life, I admit there were always touchstones and indicators along the way that I had missed. Let's take a look at yours.

Connecting the Dots

An exercise I'd recommend in this process of paying more attention to your true self (who you really are behind the curtain) is to write down those instances you can remember from childhood through young adulthood where you had a feeling of "oneness" (the only word I can use to describe it). Then you can begin to put these "dots" of self-awareness on your own life list.

The longer you're on the road to your Montage Career, the more you'll realize there's a thread connecting those kinds of moments. It may be where you're mentoring somebody and you've had a feeling of Wow, I really enjoy this! Or, Oh my gosh – I'm really good at this! And somebody wants me to do it?! Or volunteering for a charity and getting great satisfaction from the task.

Or it might be where you've helped a friend rearrange a room in their home. You may not be a professional interior decorator, but you have a knack for where things should be placed, how they'll fit together, and what colors might go well together.

Maybe you're writing the newsletter for your church or alumni association, and somebody comments on the fact that your writing is incredible. You get goosebumps because you've never really considered writing, or you've considered it but didn't know how to pursue it.

To me these are all indicators – the litmus tests that can be the map pointing the way to a remade life. Once you start putting events on your life list, it may seem like they're totally disjointed experiences (i.e., mentoring, design, organizational skills) that could be a totally diverse and non-sequential road map for your Montage Career.

But when you notice that certain experiences happen more often, the goal is to have them be a working part of what you're doing, how you're spending your time, and how you're making a living. But at the very least, they'll be an oasis where you can replenish your soul while you support yourself in some other endeavor.

Do you see a thread throughout these "dots"? Is there a recurring "theme" in what you like to do, how you like to do it, the environments you thrive in and what type of people make you feel the most "alive" when you are doing it? It's worth reviewing these "dots" over and over until you can at least tease out a rough thread that connects them. If none appears or you feel frustrated, don't stress! As you proceed on this path, the dots are more and more likely to eventually connect. For some of us, it may be many years after the fact, but if you keep your ear to the ground and listen closely, the connections will emerge and give you great clarity.

For me, the "dots" where I feel the most alive are when I'm mentoring or helping people with their creative careers. It started when I became a manager of a marketing department at the tender age of 28 and continued on until I became acutely aware of it while teaching a college class in my mid-50s. I had also felt the "pull" of this as I mentored people in a spiritual support group I've been a part of for almost 30 years. I had never connected these "dots" though until I felt the "goosebumps" of helping students in my class. It happened again during my first acting gig around the same time.

That was 11 years ago, and slowly my life has become centered around those "goosebump" moments to the point at which today I am a career and transition coach helping people live their creative dreams. As an added bonus: the on-air TV and acting work completes most of my professional "Montage".

If you get nothing else out of this book, hopefully you'll realize you'll need to take some sort of action once you gather all the information. First, you'll want to get your goals and dreams out of your head and into a practical plan you can follow to start producing results. Once you've got your plan in place, have confidence and faith that once you are in motion and taking action, other forces in the universe will conspire to take you where you need to go. Dreams without action are just dreams.

For example, as I got more in touch with this idea of doing on-air work, commercials and print modeling, the action of taking acting lessons became quite apparent as something I needed to do. About one year prior, I had signed up to take an acting class in a community college. Besides the fact I was by far the oldest person (most were 20-something would-be stars and starlets), I completely surrendered to not knowing anything about acting.

The teacher made me feel very comfortable about being a novice. She intuitively knew that I needed to set aside anything that had to do with my career in order to focus on this fun "hobby." She told me about a group she had on Sundays at a local community theater, which eventually evolved into taking classes on commercial acting.

The moral of this story is that once you step onto the carousel of your dreams, it's impossible to know the kinds of animals you'll be able to ride. But you have to get on the carousel and then stay on the ride to see what kinds of adventures you'll experience.

The process of becoming a professional actor or on-air host would never have become apparent to me sitting at home thinking or reading about it, or doing any of the passive activities people do as an alternative to taking action.

I'm not saying this was a completely wonderful experience without any bumps along the way. There were many times I wanted to stop, but something inside me said, "Look, Pat, you've started a number of projects and gotten them to a certain point. Then, for whatever reason – children, job, marriage – you've set them down and haven't picked them back up." So I became determined not to do that again with my acting and on-air projects.

One thing I encourage you to do is to define a very specific goal as the litmus test of whether it's something you want to pursue. In my case, my goal was to have a commercial agent who could get me auditions and commercials. Your specific goal could be writing a short story, finishing a painting, redecorating a friend's living room, getting a certificate at a community college or a degree at a university. Setting a deadline for pursuing your Creative YOU Turn dream will help keep you on track and prevent you from giving up before you even start. Here are a couple of ways to help your connect your own "dots" that will make this goal desirable.

Finding Your Life List

Nancy Collamer, in her great book *Second Act Careers*, has an exercise I like which asks readers to look back on the activities they've really enjoyed in their childhood, then list them and explore the ones that have carried over into their adult life. She suggests posing questions to yourself like:

- What were your favorite subjects and activities during grade school?

  _____

- What were your favorite movies?

  _____

- How did you spend your free time?

  _____

- Who were your favorite adults?

  _____

- What did you fantasize about becoming when you grew up?

  _____

- What did others think (or say) you might be when you grew up?

  _____

You can repeat this exercise focusing on your high school and college years:

- What were your favorite jobs?

  _____

- What were your least favorite jobs?

  _____

- Who were some favorite teachers?

  _____

- What was your social life like and what did you enjoy doing socially?

  _____

Finally, do this around your professional years:

- What was your favorite job?

  _____

- What was your least favorite job?

  _____

- What business-related skills do you most enjoy using?

  _____

- What were your favorite work-related accomplishments?

  _____

- Who do you want to work with? (Types of people and organizations)

  _____

- What's your ideal work environment? (Physical space or location)

  _____

Then, I have my clients add the following to Nancy's great list:

- When have you felt "goosebumps" – a sense of flow or unity in an activity or work?

  _____

- What work or play environment makes you feel at peace, unity, or closer to God or some sort of higher power?

  _____

- What type of people inspire you by simply being around them?

  _____

- What activities do you have in common with them?

_____

...Or It's in the Cards!

Another fun way to go through this "calling" process are Richard Leider's "Calling Cards".

Richard has written a number of books in this field of life re-invention that I highly recommend. "The Power of Purpose", "Repacking Your Bags" and my favorite "Life Reimagined" co-authored with Alan Webber. Richard created and produced his "Calling Cards" as a fun yet VERY effective way to discover your calling with a simple formula of:

GIFTS + PASSIONS + VALUES =CALLING

He's been nice enough to give me permission to recommend his cards and formula here and it's a fun activity to do with a partner to help start your Creative YOU Turn in a practical and specific way. You can find Richard's cards on Amazon or via his website at: www. richardleider.com

CHAPTER 9

How to Prioritize, Focus & Finish YOUR Turn

"The way to get started is to quit talking
and start doing." —Walt Disney

I'M A LOUSY SURFER. I'VE been trying on and off to become good at it for literally decades. I still suck. I'm great in the ocean at nearly everything else—I've been body surfing since I was 5, kayaking, stand-up paddle boarding, and even water skiing. All duck soup! Surfing, however, is still hard. I can do it, but it's hard.

I have two great stories about my self-loathing and outside perception of myself as a "surfer" though. What we think inside about our journey and what others think of us can be VERY different.

One happened on my honeymoon in Hawaii in 1992. I decided to give surfing another try and the hotel my new wife and I were staying in offered surfing lessons. I was out in the surf off of Kauai' with my 20-year-old teacher, trying my best and getting a few waves. He was a good teacher (and 19 years my junior).

At one point, I looked at some of the people watching from the beach and said, "Boy, I bet they're getting a good laugh watching this old guy flop around out here trying to surf!" This was typical of me around things I was not good at. I'll throw myself under the bus before you get the chance to. My guru surfing coach simply said, "Well, you're out here trying and they're just in there watching." Out of the mouths of babes! It was music to my ears…

The second story happened in Ventura, about 15 years later, as I was repeating a rather dismal attempt in the breakers. I was exhausted and started heading in. On the beach, with my board under one arm, two guys who looked like locals were walking towards me. I was sure they'd seen my humiliating performance in the choppy waves. I figured it was all they could do to conceal their giggles as they got closer.

There was no way not to acknowledge them as our paths crossed, so I said "Hi". The more grizzled surfer veteran of the two simply said, "Wow, you're my hero to be out there in that stuff, good for you!" and kept walking. Whaaat? His hero? Well, there you go.

These types of experiences in surfing taught me to stop giving a damn about being new at something and to quit thinking so much about what others are thinking about me. It was invaluable in my later forays into acting, on-air work, and improv among other pursuits. People LIKE to help those of us who are trying something new and taking a chance, so remember that and allow yourself to tap into that helpful energy as you step out on your next creative branch.

Sprinters vs. Marathon Runners

In managing, teaching, and coaching artists (at Disney and elsewhere), I've come to recognize that, by and large, creatives are often great starters and lousy finishers. I think it's the nature of the creative mind to be restless and want to start new things all the time. That's why I loved the TV and advertising industries—there was always a new product or show to LAUNCH! I love to launch, it's all the other sundry business of keeping the spacecraft in the air I find BORING. I want to simply move on to building a new spacecraft or start a new exploration.

When I was first training to become an actor and TV host, I got frustrated with my progress and started wondering if the time and effort was worth it. Fortunately, since I had a mentor and a support group, they helped me identify my "shiny object/bored/quit syndrome" pattern as just that. So I set a reasonable goal of getting a commercial agent and not even THINKING about quitting until I accomplished that. If it took a month or a year, I would stick to it. I was willing to commit to that. It ultimately took about 6 months and came about because of my mentor. She was able to introduce to me her agent who wasn't taking on any new clients but agreed to talk to me as a courtesy to my mentor. After a personal interview, she saw something in me and decided to take a chance on a relative novice. My auditions and jobs subsequently improved tenfold and led to me getting a print modeling agent. Now I do land acting and modeling gigs regularly, and none of it would have ever happened if I had listened to my own "inner voice" that wanted to quit and get the creative rush of starting something new.

Why not give yourself a break and do this all in the proper order to design a YOU turn that can succeed? I mention the proper order because I see a lot of skipping around with creatives in wanting to jump steps. This is the part where a montage is NOT like a piece you can throw together quickly. Allow the time and patience to let this new branch grow and enjoy all the bends along the way. It will allow for a strong and healthy creative tree.

The Spiritual Piece

Earlier in the book I mentioned my experience in "discovering" Marcel Duchamp in the Philadelphia Museum of Art. A feeling of peace, contentment, and excitement came over me in that moment. It was sacred in a creative sense. I'm sure you've had that feeling—that sense of "oneness"—with a piece of music or art or nature. It's exhilarating, and then we get on the freeway to drive home and it's gone. We do, however, have sense memory, which allows us to remember the sense of FLOW at a physiological level. We remember certain feelings, tastes, smells, etc. that shook us awake and made us feel alive when we experienced them and are often able to recall those profound moments.

I have had those deep and moving spiritual experiences numerous times in my life. They tend to sneak up on me like a whisper in my ear.

The first one I remember was when I was a boy of about 7 walking home from church choir practice in the little beach town of Corona del Mar, California. For some reason, I stopped and started looking up into the eucalyptus trees beside me and at once felt at peace. In that moment, I knew that life was meant to be a beautiful and wonderful thing. It was an overwhelming sense of unity at being one with the world. It's the same feeling of contentment, happiness, and joy I get when I'm attuned to my purpose in life.

It's my belief these kinds of feelings are connected to my Creative YOU Turn success. It's this process of becoming aligned in order to achieve your goals. Think of it as an internal tuning fork.

The activities by which you earn a living or create your new passions need to be in tune with what you should manifest daily in order to live a purposeful life. When I decided I wanted to become an executive career coach, I had to find mentors, training, and schools to keep me on track and achieve my goals. The same was true for acting and TV work. There was a sense of it being right "in my bones" that evolved as I took the action to achieve my YOU turn. So be thoughtful and intentional with the actions you take towards your new life, but the most important part is to act. The more actions you take, no matter how small, the less chance the heavy weight of "being stuck" will have of winning back control of your life.

By this point, you should have had an opportunity to pull some of these ideas together in writing, hopefully with your accountability buddy or magic person, so now you can launch a plan you can stick to and grow with. If, however, you still haven't gotten some goals down and/or identified a person who's willing to support you on your YOU turn, I encourage you to go back and complete the writing prompts in previous chapters then return to this point once you're ready.

Creative YOU Turn Plan Summary – *Improv-style*

You've come a long way in your Creative YOU Turn launch. Really, this Creative YOU Turn has 3 distinct stages you can think about as we review the plan and follow-up needed in order to succeed. Think of this process as a Space Launch. You're on the launch pad and I'm in Mission Control.

1. **First came the data collection on the purpose and goal of the "YOU Turn", or clarifying your destination. Remember: "Shoot for the stars, land on the moon".**

    *   So far, you've spent time defining some specifics around where you want to go and what you want to achieve creatively. (Chapter 1)_____
    *   You've created the time and space for your creative "launch pad". (Chapter 2)

        _____
    *   We've audited and rearranged some of your existing life roles to make way for your new creative goals. (Chapter 3)

        _____

2. **Second was creating a safe and supportive vehicle and test flights for your launch.**

    *   You designed and maybe even started some of the "test flights" to get things going. (Chapter 4)

        _____
    *   You found and embedded yourself into a new creative community to be a part of and flourish in. (Chapter 5) (Additional resources can be found in the back of the book if you haven't found your creative community yet.)

        _____

3. **Third, we identified the fuel and maintenance needed for your new flight and getting to your destination.**

- You created a montage revenue and budget to make this an easy career transition or viable second-act creative lifestyle. (Chapter 6)

- You identified the Magical People who can help you along the way and be your external guidance system. (Chapter 7)

- You found ways to prioritize and focused your attention on this new "flight plan" so you not only launch successfully but you guarantee safe arrival at your destination. (Chapter 8)

Now you can use the chapters and worksheets to implement a plan that will allow you to pull all these elements together in a way that's worthwhile, achievable, and sustainable. For me, this wasn't an easy process; in fact, it started way before I consciously acknowledged it was happening.

Because I was a vendor and self-employed in the entertainment industry, I was reactive in terms of the services I provided. As one skill set would become obsolete by the nature of the volatile entertainment industry, a new skill set would evolve that I'd showcase to solicit clients. A perfect example of this is when I first started out in television and I was writing ads that appeared in a newsprint pulp version of *TV Guide*. Years later, I ended up promoting *The Rachael Ray Show* on a mobile app for smart phones.

Unfortunately, the latter one didn't fly in the end, but I did a lot of work on it and I'm very proud of where it was headed. More importantly, I gained valuable new experience and a new skill set, and I had a newfound confidence because I'd accomplished something I'd never done before in terms of how promotion and marketing were changing in the digital age.

Walk Before You Run – But DO Start Walking!

As a neophyte actor, the first audition I went on was a bank commercial for Wells Fargo, and boy, was I petrified! Even though I had taken classes and had been coached and prepped on how to behave in an audition, walking into a room full of veteran actors was like stepping onto a ledge of a ten-story high-rise building.

I couldn't even remember if my teacher had told me to sign in on the "arrival list" right away and then study my lines, or study my lines and then sign in (I did the latter, which I eventually realized was the wrong choice).

There was a long wait before I was called into the actual audition room. Once inside, I didn't say hello to the director or the camera operator – I just went to my mark, faced the camera, and waited for direction. I knew enough to know that was the right protocol, and I was able to pull that off as though I had done it many times before.

I was then asked to slate my name: "Hi, I'm Pat Pattison." And when I started reading the lines on cue cards, the cameraman stopped me and said, "We're not going to do that yet. You're just slating for now." Great – I'd already made my first mistake. When he finally cued me, I read my lines to the best of my ability.

After I was thanked for my efforts, I walked out the door and practically collapsed outside. Though I was lucky to survive the audition, I didn't book the job. But in the process, I gained experience, and on the next audition I was much more self-assured. I knew where to sign in, I knew how to listen for the director to call "action!", and I had learned to show enthusiasm and talk to the camera while comfortably reading lines I'd learned only 20 seconds beforehand.

My teacher had told me, "Treat yourself every time you go to an audition." So after every audition, I've bought myself a vanilla ice cream cone, which has become my Pavlovian reward response to the very stressful moment after leaving an audition and waiting to hear whether I landed the role. Since then, I've been on hundreds of auditions and have been fortunate enough to have booked a lot of work in TV, film, and print advertising. And, for better or worse, I've eaten just as many ice cream cones.

Hearing the Director call "ACTION!"

Are you hearing a loud, urgent voice inside your head yelling "Action!"? Or maybe a quieter whisper saying "It's time"?

Your first baby steps are to create a preliminary plan to stick your toe into the ocean of your new creative career or passion. This stage might be the most important one of all, as it's where you take hold of the controls of the spacecraft and get a feel for whether you like flying. Otherwise you're just standing on the ground looking up at the sky and thinking you'd like to fly, which is an entirely different experience.

As Stan Freese pointed out, you can only practice so long, and at some point you need to start booking gigs. It's not necessarily about a particular gig, but what it can lead to.

My zigzag career went from:

• Teaching

- to a skit
- to acting lessons
- to on-camera work
- to print modeling
- and eventually saying 'yes' to executive coaching and regular TV hosting.

The director in my mind who yelled "Action!" all those years ago has yet to yell "Cut!" So, like the Energizer Bunny, I'm still going and going and going – and it's a total blast.

Now It's YOUR Turn!

So is this a steady and straight line of progress? Of course not. But if you keep your eye on the ball, it WILL give you purpose and hope even in the toughest of times, and you'll "wake up" in a place you have always wanted to be creatively.

Along the twists and turns of the zigzag were also many tough and confusing moments: my wife of many years died of breast cancer, my mother died, we weathered the Great Recession of 2008, and most recently, the COVID-19 pandemic has turned our world upside-down. No matter what happened, however, I kept remembering Martin Sheen responding "Well, I'm going to be 70 anyway!" When I let those words of Sheen's inspire me magic things happened and magic people showed up. They will show up for you too. So…

It's YOUR time for YOUR You Turn! Start it now and you'll never be sorry. Don't start and you'll always regret it.

My wonderful artist mother, Lillian, was a constant inspiration to me. She lived to be 94. On one of my last visits to see her, we were in the dining room and there we some flowers someone had sent on the table. She was on oxygen and fairly frail but could still sit at the table. She asked me to bring the flower vase closer so she could see it. I assumed she just wanted to have a better look or maybe smell a flower. When I got it close to her, though, she positioned it the way she wanted it in the light, pulled out a pad of art paper and a pencil, and started sketching it! 94 years old and creating right up until the end! That's the vision I recall whenever I'm feeling uninspired or stuck because it's the way I want to be as I continue evolving and aging creatively.

Your final task, before I set you free to go live your best creative life, is to create a lasting vision that will take you the distance. A vision that will cut through all the doubt and negative thinking. The vision that will perk you up when in a rough patch. But most of all, an image that, deep down, inspires and speaks to your innermost creative self, the one that resonates so deeply that you'd do anything to be in its presence. Mine's my mom asking for her art supplies and then sketching the flowers on her dining room table. You're welcome to borrow mine to get started (Mom would love it!), but as you progress along this journey, make it your marching orders to tap into a vision that is singular to who you are and where you want to be – whether it's the way a subject looks in a certain beautiful painting, a photograph of one of your favorite creatives in their element, or the memory you have of one of your creative mentors or heroes and the feeling you had when you were near them and they were talking to you and you alone.

Once you have your vision, hold onto it with your life. Keep it close and trust that it will guide you exactly where you were always meant to be.

Now, go on and make some magic. It's your time and YOUR TURN!